How to choose

CAR TOOLS

To Bob Horobin whose perpetual Sunday morning sojourns beneath his car inspired the start of this book, and to my wife without whose encouragement (not to mention her typing) it would never have been finished.

© J D Humphries   1974

First published August 1974

Made and printed in England by J H Haynes and Company Limited, Sparkford, Yeovil, Somerset

ISBN 0 085429 163 6

How to choose and use CAR TOOLS

John Humphries

GT Foulis

Contents

The widening interest in automobiles as a hobby as well as a means of transport, together with the rapidly escalating costs of garage work leads many car owners to tackle their own vehicle maintenance and modification. This book is written to help such car owners who lack practical experience and start off with little other than their native wit and plenty of enthusiasm.

It is intended to support, not supersede, the wealth of excellent workshop manuals and other books on car maintenance available today which give great detail on topics such as how to fit a new widget valve to your 1937 Super Aero Sports, or how to turn your Rolls-Royce into a drag racer. Notable amongst this literature is the series of manuals for individual vehicles produced by the publisher of this book.

However, all of these manuals have so much detailed information to convey in a limited space that their authors must make some assumptions about the basic skills of the reader. If you have served an engineering apprenticeship you will be all right, but for the rest of the do-it-yourself brigade, some reference to this book will be needed. It provides a lot of the basic information about the tools you will need and how to use them. It is based on twenty years experience of taking cars to bits (and in the majority of cases, getting them back together again!). Application of the hints given here can save you blood, effort, time, and probably money.

If you find yourself struggling to absorb the information contained in these pages, then do-it-yourself is probably not for you. You had better put on a resigned smile and take your car and cheque book around to your friendly neighbourhood garage. If, on the other hand, when you have read this book, you wonder what all the fuss was about — after all, its only commonsense, isn't it? — then you really have that machine in your power; able to 'tweak its revs' or 'sharpen its anchors' or whatever it is you have in mind.

A quick glance at the contents list (you passed it on a previous page) might lead you to think that this is a random selection of disconnected ideas. Well it isn't quite! After some preliminaries about safety, the materials you will be encountering and how to measure up the job, there are several chapters on fastenings and the tools needed to cope with them. After all, most work on a car seems to involve taking things apart. If this proves to be too peaceful for you, then move on to Chapters 10 to 14 which deal with cutting processes, or the even more aggressive Chapters 15 and 16, dealing with gripping and hitting. After some miscellaneous useful tools, Chapters 18 and 19 deal with the special skills needed when getting involved with the electrics. Chapters 20 to 24 then give information on various workshop 'housekeeping' type operations.

To show you how all this is applied in practice, two common beginner's jobs are described in detail: fitting reversing lights and replacing an exhaust system. The book is rounded off with information on where to get help and supplies for your activities and some 'get-you-home' tips which might help you out of a sticky corner one day.

So much for why the book was written and how it was put together. Now it is all up to you. I wish you the best of luck as you delve ever deeper into the fascinating inside of your car.

Carrying out maintenance on your car exposes you to a number of accident risks common in workshops. If you have never worked in an engineering workshop you may not anticipate these risks, which can be very different to those normally encountered at home. I make no apologies therefore for devoting the first chapter to spelling out some of the most common of these risks, even though some of these warnings will be repeated again at appropriate places later in the book.

Personal Protection

If possible, wear the right sort of clothes for the job, although if you're trying to mend a fault on the way home from a 'Grand Ball', you probably haven't much alternative to the dress suit. Preferably, your clothes should be loose enough to give you freedom of movement, but not have loose parts dangling which can catch in the works. An overall is a good thing. At least you will not have to worry about getting oil on your best shirt, which may otherwise distract your attention at some critical moment.

Sleeves should be rolled up to give your arms complete freedom of movement. It is probably wiser to remove your wristwatch too. It will save smashing it when your hand slips, as it inevitably will. Do not carry anything in top pockets where it could fall out as you lean over the works, and **never** have a loose tie dangling.

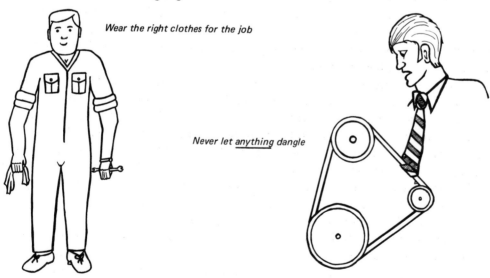

Wear the right clothes for the job

Never let anything dangle

Never carry sharp edged tools such as screwdrivers, rules, chisels, etc in your pockets. A fall can lead to very nasty injuries.

If you are going to do some rough work, such as cleaning a rusty exhaust or repairing some rough metal work, it is a good idea to wear protective gloves. They can also be a useful protection for your hands if you are lifting heavy components.

For much of the work you will be doing, gloves would be an impediment; inevitably your hands get dirty and oily and may get scratched. It is wise to rub in one of the proprietary antiseptic barrier creams before you start work. This protects against the risk of dermatitis arising from the effect of oils, from infection if the skin is broken, and makes it easier to clean the skin when you have finished work.

If you are going to carry out any work which can produce flying particles — chiselling, grinding, wire-brushing, etc — then wear some form of goggles to protect your eyes. Never gamble with your eyesight — it is much too precious.

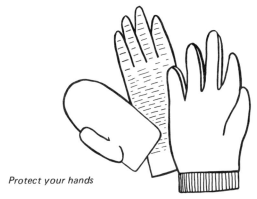

Protect your hands

Protect your eyes

Manual Lifting

Many of the parts you will be handling are heavy and have sharp edges. It is a fact that the manual handling of materials and workpieces causes more accidents in workshops than any other factor. Don't let this unhappy statistic apply to your home workshop as well. The following is a list of common accidents caused by the simple operation of lifting: crushed fingers, toes and feet; cuts and bruises to legs and arms; torn back muscles; injuries to the spine; rupture.

As a start, try to avoid lifting; whenever possible slide or roll the piece you want to move. Use levers or other aids to help you. It may take a little longer but it is probably safer. For example, a cylinder head you pick up off the bench seems fairly heavy; by the time you are stretched out over the front wing you have just about reached your limit; and by the time you have held it there for 20 seconds while you try to line it up with the studs, your fingers and arms have had enough and it slips. You have strained your back, ripped the skin on one arm, crushed a finger, and damaged the head. It is much safer to call your spouse or your neighbour to give you a hand.

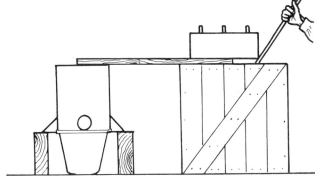

Try to avoid lifting

If you really must lift heavy weights, the following principles will limit the possibility of injury:

1   Place the feet slightly apart with one foot in front of the other.
2   Tuck your chin in and keep your back straight.

3 Bend the knees so that the powerful leg
  muscles take the strain and not the spine.
4 Tuck the elbows well in.
5 Use the palms of the hand for gripping,
  and not the fingers.
6 Lift in a smooth movement using the leg
  and thigh muscles for most of the work.
  Do not snatch.

The right way to lift

Mechanical Lifting

Be extremely careful when using any form of lifting tackle, be it a hoist, jack, or simple lever. Make sure that the equipment you are using is adequate for the job and is in good condition. If in doubt use something stronger.

Is this you?

Always allow for the lift to fail. Back it up with blocks or ensure that there is nothing beneath which will be damaged if failure occurs. This is particularly important with that most common lift for the do-it-yourself car man — jacking the car up to get under. Always think what might happen if that jack slipped.

Care should be taken when lifting greasy objects; they can slip so much easier. Clean a non-slip surface for gripping.

If lifting by a pull on some component, make sure it is strong enough to take the weight without distortion.

Never leave a load hanging from a hoist; put it down somewhere safe.

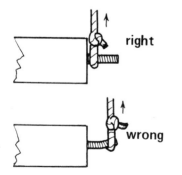

right

wrong

Make sure the lifting point is strong enough

Keep the place clean

Good Housekeeping

Keep the areas where you are working clean and tidy. Components, scrap and oil spillage on the floor all lead to the risk of falls.

Do not smoke when you are working on your vehicle — after all, you are usually pretty close to enough petrol to make a 'good bomb'. Keep a fire extinguisher readily accessible. Operations like drilling or grinding in the engine compartment or near the fuel filler can produce enough sparks to start a fire.

Dispose of your rubbish properly. Some resins and oils quite commonly used, when impregnated into some cloth can cause spontaneous combustion.

Avoid working on a running engine. When it cannot be avoided, for example when tuning a carburettor, be very careful with your clothing and tools. It is very easy to forget about the spinning fan, which tends to 'disappear' at speed.

Make sure that electrical tools are kept in good condition. Watch out for any signs of fraying of the mains lead and make sure that the earth lead is properly connected by regular checks. It seems an obvious thing to say, but it has been known to happen — don't cut through the power lead with the tool itself because of your enthusiastic concentration on the job.

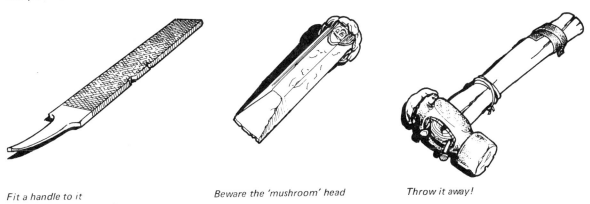

Fit a handle to it   *Beware the 'mushroom' head*   *Throw it away!*

Use and Care of Tools

Never use a file without a handle — many hands have been pierced by the sharp tang of a file.

Never use a file as a lever. The hardening process makes them very brittle and if subjected to a bending stress they are likely to snap without warning.

After extensive use, the end of a cold chisel can become 'mushroomed'. A chisel should never be used in this state as it is liable to split and fragments fly off. Always wear some eye protection when using a chisel. A hammer head must be firmly fixed to its handle and secured with a wedge. Replace a split handle immediately; never try to patch it up. If the face of a hammer becomes chipped or cracked it may split in use; get rid of it.

Always use the right size of spanner. If the jaws of a spanner become worn, either throw it away or grind them out to the next larger size. When applying a force to a spanner, make sure you are in a stable position, and whenever possible pull towards yourself. If you have to push away from you, do so with the palm of your hand. Then, if the spanner slips, it hits that sharp edge and not your knuckles.

Avoid worn spanners

When using a hacksaw, always make sure the blade is kept adequately tight. If you have been doing a lot of sawing the blade gets hot and expands and may loosen. A slack blade tends to twist and jam and will break easily. If a blade breaks when you are putting your weight behind the saw it can easily cause you to hit your hands or lose your balance.

Many hands have been pierced with a screwdriver because the object being worked on was held in the hand. Always secure the workpiece in a vice or in some other way so that you have both hands available.

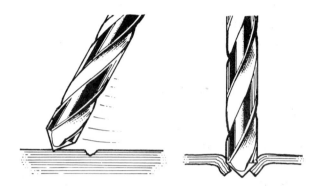

The dangerous times for drilling - when starting and finishing

When using a power drill there are two occasions of high risk. The first is when you first start a hole. If the centre marking has not been good enough, the point of the drill will jump away and you have little control over the damage it does — either to the vehicle or to you. The second is when the drill is just breaking through, particularly with large drills in thin metal. At that point the drill may 'bite in' and jam, and the power tool can twist out of your hands.

Well, no it isn't really; but because a large part of a modern automobile is made of sheet steel very little thicker than tinplate, it is not surprising that they are called 'tin boxes'. There are, however, a lot of variants of steel used, together with various other materials, and while it is unlikely that you will need to know exact specifications, a general awareness of the materials in your vehicle will help you in choosing and applying your tools.

Steel

Certainly, the most important material is steel in a multitude of different forms. Steel is made from a mixture, or 'alloy', of the element iron with small proportions of carbon and other elements. The most common form is 'mild steel' in which the carbon content lies between 0.15% and 0.25%. You may also hear reference to 'high-carbon' or 'tool' steel, in which the carbon content is in the range 0.45% to 1.50%. The other main group is the 'alloy steels' which have had added one or more of elements such as tungsten, chromium, cobalt, vanadium, manganese, silicon and nickel to give various special properties. For example, the 'stainless steels' generally contain a good proportion of nickel.

The engineer is interested in a number of properties of the material he is using. The ductility of the material affects his ability to form it into the finished shape — for example a complex curve in a body panel. The strength and toughness govern the load the material can withstand and its ability to absorb shock. The hardness is important for wearing surfaces such as bearings. By choosing the various alloys the engineer can find the best mix of properties to meet a particular need.

Metallurgical Processes

However, these properties are also affected by the way the material is processed. Steel is first produced in a molten state at high temperature. If it is then poured into a mould and allowed to cool it will solidify into the shape of the mould and one has a steel casting. For producing complex shapes this process is very attractive, but in the finished state the steel consists of microscopic crystals arranged rather like the crystals in a lump of sugar. In this form the material is very brittle and has limited strength. Modern techniques have now been developed which produce steel castings good enough to be used for heavily loaded components like crankshafts, but these are still rare.

Much of the steel produced is poured into simple rectangular 'ingot' moulds, and when solidified passed on to further processes where it is either squeezed between rollers or hammered in presses to produce the finished product. From the rolling mills come all the steel sheets, rods, bars, girders and other continuous shapes which are the everyday materials of the engineer. Not only does the rolling process produce the shape required, the 'mechanical working' changes the crystalline structure of the metal into a fibrous one, similar to the structure of wood or muscle. This greatly enhances the strength and ductility of the finished product.

If this already 'worked' material is taken and further squeezed or hammered between dies in a press, the end product becomes a forging. In this, not only has the material been generally

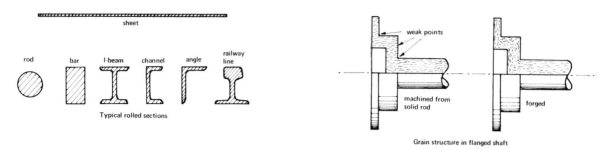

Typical rolled sections

Grain structure in flanged shaft

strengthened further, but the grain structure in the metal is caused to follow the contours of the finished object, thereby eliminating 'cross-grain' weak spots.

Even these different production processes do not exhaust the possibilities for the metallurgist. He also has available 'heat treatment'. By heating and cooling the material, either generally or locally, through a range of temperatures and at differing rates, the grain structure can be further modified to give different properties. The simplest form of heat treatment was by the blacksmith who, having forged a sword, would heat the edge to a bright red heat and then quench it in a barrel of water. This would give a very hard edge which could be sharpened to cut through the toughest armour. In the modern automobile equivalent an engine crankshaft is forged to give a uniformly tough material which will withstand the shock loads imposed during running. It is then rapidly heated and quenched to give a hard non-wearing surface for the bearing points.

Uses of Steel

How then are these processes likely to have been applied in your vehicle? Castings are likely to be used for the main engine block, cylinder head, gearbox and clutch casings and for other complex but lightly stressed components. Most of the heavily stressed working parts of the engine are likely to be heat-treated forgings as will be usually the components of the vehicle suspension. The remaining steel parts will be made from flat sheet, bar or rod, in many cases by pressing into shape and welding together.

The implications of these various processes for your do-it-yourself maintenance are not many, but they are important. Components which have a high surface finish, part of the main power train, are obviously forgings or likely to be highly stressed, should be treated with the greatest care. They should never be cut, drilled or subjected to heat unless you have very carefully studied what you are working with and have taken appropriate advice.

Modern automobiles are very sophisticated devices, and the safety factor, or 'spare capacity', of many components is quite small. While they can be very reliable as originally designed and built, any alteration from the designed condition could lead to catastrophic failure. Even a scratch on the surface of a forging can reduce its ultimate strength, and in racing cars it is common practice to polish components to a mirror finish to remove any possible weakness. Production vehicles of course are designed to a much poorer finish, but care still needs to be taken. Perhaps the most likely place for error is when working in the vicinity of the front suspension. It could be that when sawing some adjacent non-stressed component, the saw slips and marks one of the main suspension links. This scratch could form the focal point for stress corrosion resulting in a failure perhaps some months later.

When working with castings, you should remember how brittle they are. Do not hit them or drop them, as they may just crack across. Screws threaded into castings should always be treated with care. It is very easy to overstress the thread and have it break away.

For the rest of the 'tin-ware' you have considerable freedom, but if you plan to start cutting large holes, remember that even the body panels on a modern automobile carry some of the stresses on the vehicle. In general, minor drilling and cutting are no problem, but if you plan to alter a significant proportion of the material in a component (say, more than 5%), give careful thought to the effect you may be having on the strength of the component.

Corrosion

One of the biggest enemies of steel is corrosion. Iron slowly oxidises in the presence of air, and the addition of water enormously accelerates the process, leading rapidly to a heap of rust. Some alloy steels are sufficiently resistant to rusting that they are referred to as 'stainless', but these are a rarity on the average vehicle. The main defence is therefore, at least to exclude moisture, and preferably to exclude air as well. The usual methods are immersion in oil (as with gears), grease, bonding another non-corroding material to the surface (some aluminium or plastic coated steels), or the most common of all, paint. Remember, whatever work you are doing, never leave bare steel surfaces exposed to the atmosphere for more than a few hours.

Work-hardening

If you have to straighten out a crunched wing, or need to do some other metal reforming job, you will find yourself encountering the phenomenon of 'work-hardening'. If you hammer or bend or otherwise 'work' steel (and many other metals) it becomes harder and more brittle and eventually will break. If you take a piece of mild steel and bend it through 90° and then straighten it out, you will see a fine pattern of cracks begin to appear at the bend point. If the bending and straightening is repeated, it is likely to fail altogether after three or four bends. This means that you have to achieve your desired result (such as a nice smooth wing panel) with the minimum amount of 'work'. In some cases this may not be feasible, the material having hardened even before you start. In this case it is necessary to 'anneal', or soften, the metal. In the case of steel this is achieved by heating until it glows red and then allowing it to slowly cool in air.

So far all the discussion has been about steel, but there are of course other materials used in an automobile, both metal and non-metal, and it is appropriate now to note some of the special characteristics of the most important ones.

Non-ferrous Metals

Aluminium and its alloys are used in some vehicles for body panels, for engine and gearbox castings and for pistons. Most of the comments made on steel are applicable here, but with the following special factors. The relative softness of aluminium makes it easy to work, but presents problems where threads are cut into it. These can be 'stripped out' very easily by careless tightening of screws. When drilling or cutting aluminium remember that in finely powdered form it is inflammable and if ignited burns with a very intense heat. Aluminium powder is one of the fillings for incendiary bombs! Aluminium is free from rusting problems, but it is attacked by strong alkali solutions.

Copper is commonly used for all electrical wiring in the vehicle. Like many other metals it is affected by work-hardening and this often happens at terminal points. If a wire is inadequately supported and subjected to vibration, the continual flexing at the terminal can result in the metal crystallising and snapping off — a common cause of wiring faults.

Brass is an alloy of copper, zinc and tin, and is often used in conjunction with copper for radiators and other cooling system components because of its good thermal conductivity and relative freedom from corrosion. It is also used for many electrical components. It is a fairly easy material to work, requiring no special actions.

Die-castings

If zinc is alloyed with bismuth, antimony and various other exotic elements, metals with a very fine grain structure and low melting point can be produced. These are the 'die-casting' alloys which are injected in liquid form under high pressure into steel moulds (or 'dies') to produce complex castings with a very smooth and accurate finish which often require no further machining before use. They are used very extensively in automobiles, wherever a lightly stressed but complicated component needs to be produced cheaply. Examples can be found in door latches, window winders, locks, carburettors, instrument housings, lamp housings, etc. Like all castings, they are brittle and being soft metals are easily marked and damaged and should be treated with care.

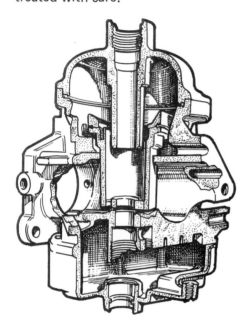

Typical die-casting

Plastics

Many functions traditionally fulfilled with die-cast alloys are now being met with plastics, and this seems an appropriate moment to comment on them. There is an enormous range of materials grouped under the title 'plastics',* including rigid and flexible materials, moulded shapes and flat sheets. The majority are associated with decorative trimmings, but increasingly they are beginning to move into the 'engineering' of vehicles. They are easy to work with, often requiring only woodworking tools. One important feature which characterises almost all of them is that they do not like heat; so be careful what you do with that blowlamp or soldering iron, and keep plastics away from the exhaust pipe and other very hot engine parts.

In some cases plastics materials are combined with a fibrous or other form of filler to give a mixture or sandwich which is stronger than either component alone. The most common example of this is the combination of epoxy resins and chopped up glass fibres to give the material commonly known as 'fibreglass'. Used for complete body shells of some specialist vehicles, its greater relevance for you is probably as a repair material for damaged steel panels. This is discussed further in Chapter 23.

Rubber

Finally, we have rubber; both in its natural form and synthetic forms such as Neoprene. The two main applications are of course tyres and hosepipes, although smaller quantities will be

* The word 'plastics' is usually used in its singular 'plastic'. Plastics is, in fact, technically correct.

found in suspension joints and buffers, anti-vibration mountings, diaphragms in pumps and fluid seals. If you have occasion to cut rubber, you will find that water as a lubricant will ease the job. When exposed to the atmosphere, and particularly to sunlight, rubber decomposes. The time taken varies with the particular rubber compound and the degree of exposure, but serious weakening and embrittlement can occur within eighteen months in some cases and any exposed rubber component more than three years old should be treated with suspicion. The most likely components to be affected by this deterioration are the cooling system hosepipes.

Water hoses deteriorate!

Once you have decided the job you are going to do, there is a temptation to dive straight in with saw or drill or hammer, only to find out afterwards that you have cut off more than you should have, or you have drilled a hole in the wrong place. Always size up the job carefully before you pick up the tools. Plan carefully what you are going to do; measure the work and mark it out accurately; offer up a new component and make sure it looks as if it will fit. If the job you are going to tackle looks at all complicated, draw it all out on paper first. This doesn't mean that you have to be a skilled draughtsman; even a sketch on the back of an old envelope will often be enough to clarify your thoughts. This can be especially important when planning alterations or additions to the electrical wiring.

Measures

For a start you are going to need a rule. No, not a child's wooden ruler. Splash out and buy yourself a decent engineer's steel rule. You will find it an invaluable tool; not just as a length measurer but also as a straight edge. You need a 12 inch one at least, and a 6 inch one can be useful for working in awkward corners. Get one that has both inch and metric graduations; you are quite likely to find yourself dealing with both. Take care of your rule; it will be your reference standard for many operations. Never let it get rusty or bent, or develop chipped and worn edges.

A well cared for broad steel rule can also be used as a square for jobs that do not require too great an accuracy, but a solid steel engineer's try-square will be needed if you plan any major works.

To help on the bigger jobs you will also need a tape measure. One of the 6 feet spring steel type is probably the most useful.

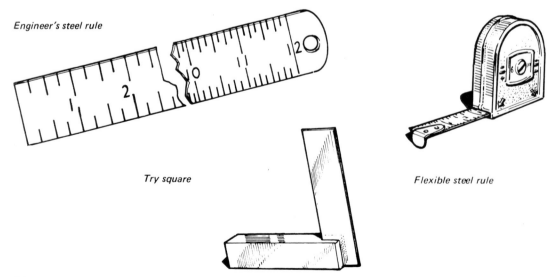

Engineer's steel rule

Try square

Flexible steel rule

Marking tools

For roughly marking work points, a soft pencil or chalk are useful, but when you come to the final marking out you need to use a scriber. This is made from hardened steel, ground to a sharp point and usually knurled on the body to provide a firm grip. They are available in simple straight single ended form, double ended straight, double ended with one end bent at right angles, and a pocket type where the point unscrews and can be tucked safely inside the body. Any type will meet your simple needs — a good sharp point. You can even make your own if you are that keen.

With the aid of the steel rule and the scriber you can mark out straight lines on your work piece that will not rub off or move. If you have some complicated marking out to do, it can sometimes be difficult to see all your scribed lines. The traditional engineer's solution for this problem, particularly on light coloured or polished metal is to coat the surface with 'engineer's blue', which is a metal dye which can be rubbed on. The scribed lines then show up bright against this darker background. Alternatively, on a dark surface, rub it over with chalk or whitewash. In many cases of course the material will be painted and the scribed lines will be easily seen. Remember the permanence of these marks and do not put them where they will show after the job is finished if you can possibly avoid it.

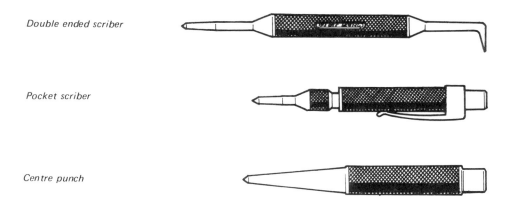

Double ended scriber

Pocket scriber

Centre punch

Another basic marking-out tool you will need is the centre punch. It is a short knurled cylinder which is brought to a strong hard point at one end. Placed against metal and hit with a hammer it leaves a small indentation. These dents or 'pop-marks' are sometimes used to identify key points on scribed lines, and will always be used to locate the centre of a hole which is to be drilled. A version known as an 'automatic centre punch' contains a spring driven hammer internally and is simply pressed by hand against the place to be marked. This compresses the spring which at the end of its travel is released to provide a uniform blow to the actual punch point.

Another useful basic tool is the divider. This consists of a pair of steel legs, with hardened points, hinged together and adjustable in their separation by a screw. It is used for transferring

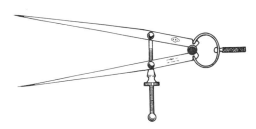

Dividers

measurements from one place to another, and for scribing circles. Indeed, it can be used instead of a scriber for drawing straight lines as well, although the simple straight scriber is sufficiently cheap to be not worth economising on.

Marking out

Well, having collected your basic tools there are a few points to be noted before you try your hand at marking out a job. The first concerns the important question of tolerances. In practice no measurement can be made with perfect accuracy, nor can any cutting operation. Inevitably then, there is some chance that the finished position of, say, a sawcut or a drilled hole will have an error from the desired position. The size of this possible error will depend on the tools available and the skill of the operator. In a precision machine shop with highly skilled operators, errors of less than one thousandth of an inch can be maintained regularly. In your garage, with hand tools, you will be lucky if you can keep to the nearest sixty-fourth of an inch, and your errors can be even greater.

You must therefore estimate your probable degree of error and make provision for it when marking out the work. To illustrate this point, consider two examples. In the first case you have a piece of steel bar 2 inches wide, ¼ inch thick and 2 feet long, and you require a piece exactly 3½ inches long. Unless you have a lot of experience, it is unlikely that you could saw through a piece of this cross section without the saw wandering up to one sixteenth of an inch. You should therefore mark two lines across the bar; one for the finished length of 3½ inches and another at 3 9/16 inches for the sawing reference. After cutting, file the rough end of the bar down to the final size needed.

For the second example, consider the requirement to mount a component which has two 3/8 inch studs protruding from it, onto a 1/8 inch thick steel panel. To make sure the component does not move on its mounting, you may decide to drill holes with the smallest possible clearance and you perhaps choose a drill of 25/64 inch diameter (1/64 inch oversize) for the job. However, with a drill of this size, on 1/8 inch thick steel and using a hand held drilling machine, you would be lucky to hold the finished position of a hole within 1/32 inch either side of the marked out point. The drill size would therefore need to be at least 13/32 inch to be sure of being able to fit the component without having to file out the holes.

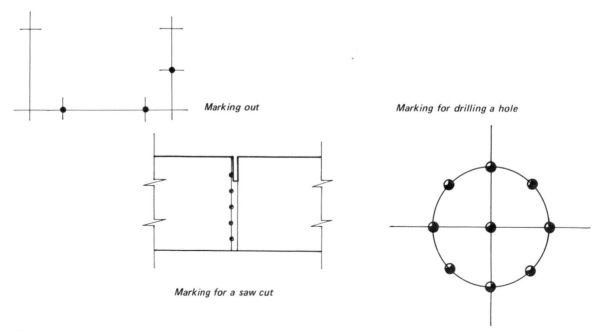

Marking out

Marking for drilling a hole

Marking for a saw cut

When marking out a job, corners and the centres of holes and other centre points are identified by scribing two short lines which intersect at right angles. If the point is to be used as a reference for many other measurements, or if it is the centre of a hole to be drilled, it should also be marked with a 'centre-pop' at the intersection of the scribed lines.

Where a saw-cut is to be made, do not forget to make allowance for the thickness of the blade. Never try to cut along the scribed line; always at one side. If accuracy is required, scribe a pair of lines separated by the width of the saw blade, and make a number of light 'centre-pop' indentations at intervals along the finished size line.

For a hole to be drilled, a substantial indentation is required at the centre. Where the hole is large and accuracy is important, scribe a circle at the full diameter as a reference guide. This technique is dealt with in greater detail in Chapter 10, 'Making Holes'.

The way in which you will find engineering drawings dimensioned takes into account the relationship between those dimensions. Consider the two ways shown here of dimensioning three holes in relation to the edges of a plate. In the first case the holes appear to have no relationship. In the second case it is obvious that the three holes are related together. The most important dimensions are probably their spacing from each other; these are linked to a common reference centre-line which is itself positioned relative to the edges of the plate.

Where a pattern of related dimensions is repeated, for example, mountings for a number of identical components, the preparation of a template can save time in marking out and improve accuracy. The preparation of a template can also be useful when dealing with a complex shape; for example the bending and cutting of a new brake pipe.

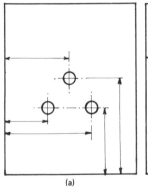
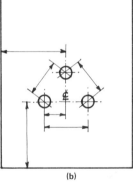

(a)   (b)

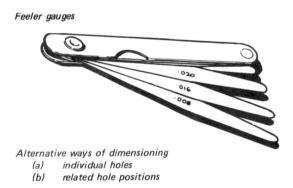

Feeler gauges

Alternative ways of dimensioning
(a)   individual holes
(b)   related hole positions

Feeler gauges

The tools and techniques discussed in this Chapter so far will cover the majority of your needs for measuring and marking out. There is however one other type of measurement which you will have to make regularly — the measurement of small gaps and clearances. The most common ones are for spark plug electrode and distributor contact breaker gaps, and valve/rocker clearances. The basic tool for this job is the feeler gauge. This consists of a thin strip of hardened steel of an exact known thickness. For some regular purposes a special gauge of the finished size required is available. Some distributor and spark plug manufacturers supply such single size gauges, sometimes in the form of a wire instead of a flat strip.

However, you will certainly require a general purpose set of feelers. These are available as a number of different thickness gauges hinged together at one end in a protective case. The sizes of the feelers are such that by selecting appropriate combinations, measurements can be made in one thousandth of an inch steps from, say, 0.003 inch to 0.100 inch.

To measure the size of a gap, select a likely looking combination of feelers by eye and attempt to insert them into the gap. If they will not enter, reduce the thickness of the gauge. If they slip in loosely, increase the thickness. At the correct setting the feelers should just move in the gap with a small amount of drag. Be careful when measuring something like a contact breaker gap where one side is spring mounted. The pressure on the feeler gauge may be enough to lift the contact against the spring, giving you a false indication of a larger gap. It is always wise to check a measurement with a gauge setting two thousandths of an inch larger and smaller to ensure that in one case there is free entry and in the other no entry.

When dealing with surfaces which may be worn, such as valve stems or contact breaker points, be careful not to be misled when measuring clearance. If the feeler gauge is passed right through the gap a false reading can be obtained if one of the faces is indented (see diagram).

Other measuring tools

If you should really decide to start doing major modifications to your automobile, there are a number of other measuring tools you could need; in any case you may come across references to their use. They are therefore briefly described here, just to round off this Chapter. The detailed techniques of their use will be found in any engineer's workshop practice textbook; if you need these tools you will need such a textbook.

Firstly there are calipers — inside and outside. Calipers are pairs of hinged legs used in conjunction with a rule for measuring the sizes of objects and spaces, particularly round ones.

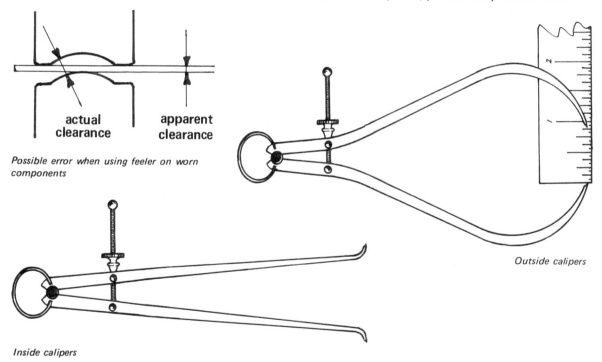

actual clearance   apparent clearance

Possible error when using feeler on worn components

Outside calipers

Inside calipers

A more refined tool for the same basic purpose is the vernier gauge which can measure up to 10 times more accurately than calipers and rule. Outside measurements are made between the lower two jaws, one of which is part of the fixed rule and the other slides on the rule. Inside measurements are made with the outside faces of the jaws where a fixed minimum dimension must be added onto the reading on the scale. The combination of the vernier scale and the main scale together permit measurement to one tenth of the minimum division on the main scale.

For even more accurate measurements one requires a micrometer, which gives about another 10 times greater accuracy. The micrometer is based on the simple idea of a very accurately made, fine pitch screw. Counting the number of turns and fractions of a turn of the screw gives accurate information about the position of its end.

The basic outside measurement micrometer is illustrated and the usual version of such an instrument will be calibrated in thousandths of an inch. Versions are also available for the internal measurement of openings and for measuring the depth of blind holes. Micrometers are available in many sizes, usually in 1 inch steps.

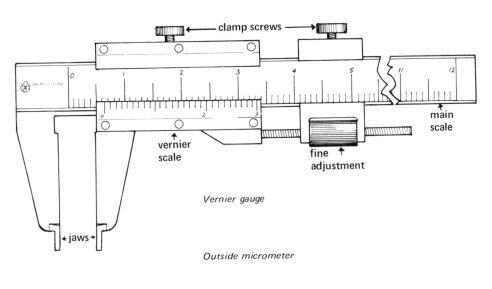

Vernier gauge

Outside micrometer

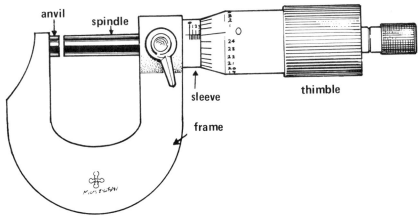

Chapter 5 Nuts, Bolts and Screws

Having disposed of the preliminaries, we now get down to the nuts and bolts — literally. The screw thread is a fundamental element in all engineering construction. Its application in the form of nuts, bolts, screws and studs is the basis of assembly of devices which must be capable of being dismantled again.

The basic definitions

What then is the screw thread? The origin of the screw is the simple wedge. The big step forward came when some unknown person conceived the idea of bending the wedge around into a spiral so that an inclined plane of indefinite length was possible. Over the centuries this became refined to the present style which consists of a cylinder with a spiral projection on the outside and a mating hole with a corresponding spiral groove on the inside. By rotating one relative to the other, the cylinder can be moved axially and is capable of exerting a force many times that required to turn it.

Many different thread forms have been developed, each to meet a particular type of load or type of material. These subtle differences are hardly relevant to your interests. They can all be considered as a V-form in cross-section (see diagram) usually with rounded top and bottom. The male and female threads have slightly different root and peak diameters so that a small clearance exists at the tips of the threads.

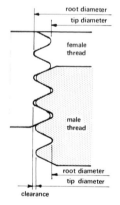

Basic thread characteristics

This basic thread structure is applied in a number of ways. Firstly, take a metal rod with a head at one end and a thread along part of the other end. This is a bolt. Now take a piece of metal formed in such a way that a rotational force can be applied to it; make a hole through and cut a matching thread on the inside of the hole. This is a nut. By passing the threaded end of the bolt through a hole in components which are to be fastened together and then screwing a nut on the other end, a firm joint can be made.

If the bolt is threaded all the way up to the head it becomes a screw (often a setscrew) although there is a popular habit of applying the word only to those screws with slotted heads (see next).

If the rod has not got a head but is threaded at both ends, it is a stud. In this form it can be

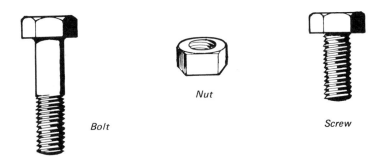

Nut

Bolt

Screw

used with two nuts to hold components together, but the usual application of the stud has one end screwed direct into a component and a nut used on the free end.

Screws are commonly used blind, being entered into a threaded hole in a component, without the use of a nut.

Nuts, bolts and screws are available in a variety of metals; steel and brass being the most common. Some steel bolts are made from special alloys and have high strength and other special properties. These are usually indicated by code letters forged on the head and fastenings of this type should not be replaced by ordinary unmarked bolts or nuts.

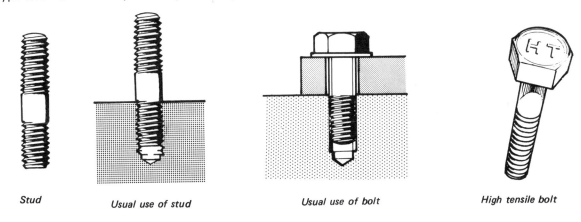

Stud

Usual use of stud

Usual use of bolt

High tensile bolt

Types of thread

It was mentioned previously that many different thread forms have been developed and these are combined with a range of standard diameters and thread pitch (the number of threads per inch) into named 'thread systems'. Fastenings from one system will not normally mate correctly with those from another. If you find that a nut which appears to be the right size gets very tight after about 1½ to 2 turns onto the male thread, the chances are that they belong to different systems. If you force the nut on you will probably strip off the thread altogether.

The following list covers the systems you are most likely to discover in your work.

British Standard Whitworth (BSW)

One of the oldest engineering threads. Not normally used on automobiles now, but may be found on some old vehicles where a coarse thread was required, such as for screwing into aluminium, and some castings.

Unified National Coarse (UNC)

An American standard coarse thread used now in automobiles for the duties of the old BSW.

British Standard Fine (BSF)

A finer pitch version of BSW which was used widely on British automobiles for general fastenings. Now almost completely superseded.

Unified National Fine (UNF)

An American fine pitch thread which has been adopted as a standard for many years throughout the American and British automobile industries. For general use.

Metric (MM)

The standard system used in European engineering and now becoming much more widespread with the gradual adoption of metric standards internationally. For general use.

British Association (BA)

A thread system particularly suited to small diameters and non-ferrous metals. Very commonly used for electrical apparatus.

In general, thread sizes are quoted as the outside diameter of the male thread. Occasionally (particularly with UNF and UNC), an A/F size will be quoted. This is the size 'across the flats' of a standard hexagon head on the particular bolt or nut; ie the size of spanner needed to turn it. BA threads are designated by size numbers, the smaller numbers being the largest in diameter. The largest size is OBA which is about a ¼ inch diameter, and the odd numbers are not used very often. Over the range of sizes you are likely to encounter on your car, the inch size threads are available in 1/16 inch steps in the diameter, while the metric ones are available in 2 mm steps.

Types of head

Bolts and screws come in a wide variety of head shapes, each of which has been developed to meet a particular class of need. Ones which you may encounter are listed.

Hexagon

The most common of all in engineering work. The head has a flat face towards the thread but is chamfered on the free end to avoid sharp corners. The diameter of the thread, the distance across the flats of the hexagon and the thickness of the head are all related by standard formulae for each thread system.

Hexagon head

Square head

Coach bolt head

Cheese head

Square

Occasionally encountered where the available space to accommodate the head is restricted, or where the head slides into a slot which stops the bolt from turning.

Coach bolt

Where the mimimum protrusion is required on the outside of an assembly, or where it is important that the fastening cannot be undone from one end (eg mounting a door lock mechanism). The square beneath the head is located in a socket formed in the component being fastened and prevents the bolt from turning when being tightened up.

Cheese

A commonly used head in the shape of a traditional cheese, for smaller screws. Rotation is by a flat screwdriver blade.

Round

A smoother, more compact screw head. Not quite as strong as the cheese head.

Countersunk

Used where there must be no projection of the head above the finished surface.

Oval

A compromise between the round and countersunk heads which is used where minimum projection is required but the component being fastened is too thin to accept a full countersunk hole.

Round head

Countersunk head

Oval head

Allen or socket

In this type of head an internal hexagon socket is formed in the head, into which a hexagon bar (Allen key) can be fitted for use as a spanner. The socket type is usually available in cheese head or countersunk styles. The cheese head is usually knurled on the outside to give a finger grip for turning when the screw is loose.

Phillips/Posidriv

In this type of head a star-shaped indentation is made in the head to take the driving tool. This type of head was originally developed to accept power driven tools without the risk of jumping out of the screw slot, which tended to characterise the old style flat blade driver. The original style was the Phillips, but more recently the Posidriv was introduced which has a different shape to the shoulders of the star to give even better non-slip driving characteristics. The makers claim that the tools are not interchangeable, but unless you are dealing with a lot of large, heavily loaded screws, you can probably get by with only one type of driver.

This type of drive is usually found on round and countersunk heads.

Cheese socket head

Countersunk socket head

Phillips/Posidriv head

Countersunk Phillips/Posidriv head

Types of nut

Nuts also come in a wide variety of shapes, each with its own function.

Hexagon

Again the most common; it is a duplicate in shape and size to the hexagon bolt head.

Hexagon lock or half-nut

A nut which is half the standard thickness of the hexagon nut and is chamfered on both sides. Sometimes used where space is restricted, it is primarily used as a back-up for locking a full nut (see later in this Chapter). When used by itself, it has only half the strength of a standard nut and can be overloaded easily.

Cap

Used where the end of a thread must be protected, either against dirt and damage, or for decorative reasons.

Hexagon nut

Hexagon half nut

Cap nut

Wing

Used where the nut must be capable of being tightened and released by hand without the use of tools.

Spring

A type of nut often used for fastening automobile trim. It does not need to be screwed all the way down the thread, but can simply be pushed on, springing over the threads. A final turn of the screw locks it tight, and it is fairly vibration proof. They are not very strong, relying normally on only part of two threads to hold, and they are rarely seen in the actual 'works'.

Castellated

Very commonly used for fastenings which **must not** come undone accidentally. The nut is first screwed on and tightened up to the required pressure. A hole is then drilled right through the screw or bolt in line with a pair of the castellations of the nut. A split pin is then passed right through nut, bolt and then the nut again, and finally bent over. The nut can now unscrew only by shearing through the pin.

Wing nut

Spring nut

Castle nut

Locking a castle nut

Split collar

Another type of nut (sometimes called an aero-nut) used to avoid the risk of unscrewing as a result of vibration. The thread runs right through the body and the collar of the nut. The collar is cut with fine overlapping slots from each side. When this is done the threads in the collar close up a little and will grip the screw quite firmly when it passes through.

Fibre collar

A similar result is obtained with this type of nut which has a fibre ring fitted inside the collar. As the nut is screwed onto a bolt, a thread is cut in the inside face of the fibre ring and it grips the bolt firmly. Nuts of this type should be used only once, as the gripping effect may not be reliable on successive occasions.

Nylon insert

Another variant on the self-locking nut (sometimes called a nyloc nut). Here a small piece of nylon or similar plastic is inserted through the side of an otherwise standard nut. As the nut is screwed on, the protruding tip of the insert is moulded to fill the clearance space between male and female threads and provides the anti-vibration grip. Again, this type of nut should be used only once.

Split collar nut

Fibre collar nut

Nylon insert nut

Special screws

As well as the standard nuts, bolts and screws already discussed, there are two special classes of screw which you will encounter.

The first are the grub or setscrews. These are used to locate a pulley or similar component on a shaft. They have a conical point which will bite into the shaft, and are headless so that they may be screwed below the surface of the component. They may have either a simple straight driving slot or a hexagon socket drive.

The second special class are the self-tapping screws which can be used to screw into a simple drilled hole without any preliminary thread cutting. They are very commonly used for attaching decorative trim on automobiles. They are really applicable only to thin or soft materials and are not very strong. They come in two basic styles.

The first looks very much like a woodscrew except that its taper is at the end followed by a parallel section rather than a uniform taper. These are used with thin and/or soft materials. A hole is drilled about the diameter of the core of the screw (at the root of the thread) and the narrow end of the screw entered into the hole. As the screw is turned the hardened thread rolls the material of the plate and forces it outwards into a thread form into which finally the parallel portion screws.

The second type is used with thicker and harder materials. It does not taper to a complete point and on one side of the taper a groove is cut which forms a cutting edge. The screw therefore becomes a combined simple thread cutting tool followed by an integral screw.

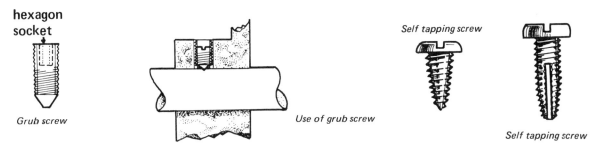

hexagon socket

Grub screw

Use of grub screw

Self tapping screw

Self tapping screw

Washers

As a hexagon nut or screw is being tightened up, the corners of the hexagon bearing against the component being clamped tend to gouge into the component. To prevent this damage, a replaceable plain 'washer' is introduced between them. The plain washer is a simple circle of metal with a hole in the centre large enough to slip over the screw or bolt. The size of hole, outside diameter and thickness are all related by standard formulae to the size of bolt, and washers are available in all the materials which are used for nuts and bolts, plus some others.

In addition to this basic function, washers are also used to cover up in situations where a very large tolerance has been given on a hole size. They are also used to spread the load where the item being fastened has a soft surface. In these latter cases the washers may be larger in diameter than standard. Washers in softer materials such as rubber, fibre or plastic will also be found, usually where it is necessary to provide a fluid seal for a thread. The washer is then strictly speaking a gasket (see Chapter 8).

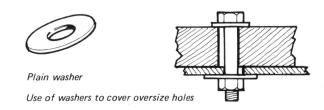

Plain washer

Use of washers to cover oversize holes

There are also a number of types of washer designed to deal specifically with locking nuts and screws against vibration. They all work on the basis of some form of spring which allows the fastening to be easily tightened but as soon as it tends to loosen the washer digs into the metal and maintains a restraining force.

The oldest form is the simple Grover single turn spring washer which is still regularly used on larger fastenings. You may come across a two turn version of this which gives more spring and therefore greater tolerance on the tightening. Used widely on smaller sizes of screws are the internal and external star washers which rely on multiple spring claws to hold against vibration.

Grover lock washer and its use

Spring lock washer

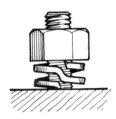

External star lock washer

Internal star lock washer

Locking

Quite a number of locking devices have already been mentioned, but the subject is worth more expansion. This pre-occupation with anti-vibration locking is absolutely vital on any automobile and you forget about it at your peril. It is amazing how rapidly a nut subjected to the right frequency of vibration can unscrew, even when apparently pulled up really tightly initially. It may take only minutes; so a steering mechanism nut replaced without its locking feature today could easily cost you your life before tomorrow.

The locking devices rely on one or a combination of two techniques. The first is to increase the friction between male and female thread, or between screw head and component, to a very high value, while the second is to create actual physical interlocks between the parts.

While a screw is being tightened up the clearance between the threads allows it to be turned quite easily. As soon as it begins to apply pressure the threads are forced together with a rapidly increasing load. As the friction forces are proportional to load one obvious answer is to just tighten up further. There are, however, two limits to this. The increasing frictional force opposes the tightening up as much as it does the untightening, and in addition you may simply break the threads. The biggest weakness of this approach is that if the screw moves back only a small fraction, the load on the thread drops immediately and any locking effect is lost. If the screw is holding a resilient component, say a padded decorative lining, reliance on the natural friction of the screw may be quite acceptable, and several of the locking techniques try to exploit this effect.

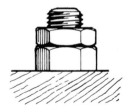

Use of a half nut for locking

Spring washers (particularly the double turn ones) and star washers all rely on keeping the pressure on the thread faces as well as trying to achieve an actual mechanical interlocking. The use of the half nut as a locking device also works on the same principle. A nut is first tightened down and is then followed by a back-up half nut. If the main nut moves in a direction which would release the pressure from the component, it simply increases the pressure from the half-nut. The biggest weakness of this arrangement is of course seen in the question — What stops the half-nut from unscrewing? The split collar nut works in a similar manner and has the advantage over some of the other anti-vibration nuts in that it can be used repeatedly.

The insert type nuts simply rely upon increasing the overall thread friction and maintaining a resilient grip which is not easily shaken by vibration. The equivalent of the plastic insert type nut can be obtained by the use of a compound (sold under names such as Loctite or Torqueseal) which is coated on the screw thread before the nut is fitted. The compound dries to hold the nut firmly against vibration.

The spring washers attempt to create a metal to metal interlock to oppose any unscrewing action and they can be particularly effective with non-ferrous metals where the difference in hardness between the spring teeth and the metal surface allows the teeth to bite well in.

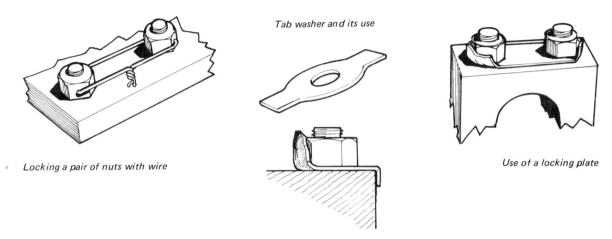

Tab washer and its use

Locking a pair of nuts with wire

Use of a locking plate

Where a fastening just **must not** come undone accidentally, positive interlocking becomes necessary. The castellated nut has already been referred to. Another similar technique is to drill a hole right through nut and threaded stem, after tightening up, and then fasten a piece of pliable but tough steel wire through the hole. A very commonly used technique with hexagon headed fastenings is the tab washer. For this a specially shaped washer is used which has two or more tabs protruding from its outer diameter. This is placed under the nut or screw head in such a way that one tab can be bent over an edge of the component being fastened or bent into a specially cut recess. After tightening the fastening, the other tab is then bent up and hammered flat against the hexagon of the nut or screw head. A variant on this theme is used when two or more adjacent heads have to be locked. In this case a loose plate is fitted across all the fastenings and after tightening, the corners of the plate are bent up to hold the hexagons. This technique will be found to be very commonly adopted on the twin screws holding bearing caps.

The spanner, or the American wrench, is the tool used with hexagon nuts, bolts and screws for tightening and untightening them. Spanners come in a variety of types and a wide range of sizes, and although apparently such simple tools there are still quite a number of tricks to be learnt about them. They are generally made of steel although this ranges from cheap mild steel to expensive high tensile, stainless alloy steel. The high strength spanners are much slimmer and easier to use in awkward corners and are worth buying.

Spanner sizes

The range of spanner sizes corresponds to the range of bolt sizes in a particular thread system. Two methods of marking are used. In one case the actual distance between the jaws of the spanner is given; the 'across the flats' dimension of a hexagon nut or bolt head. It is indicated by a dimension followed by the letters A/F (eg 5/16 inch A/F). This is quite common for spanners intended for use with 'Unified' system nuts and bolts.

The other method gives the bolt diameter in a particular system for which the spanner fits the head. Usually the size is followed by an indication of the system (eg 7/16 inch BSF; 36 MM), but sometimes only the dimension is given. You will also find multiple references to different thread systems and combinations of bolt diameter and A/F measurements. All very confusing! In the end your only safeguard is actually to fit the spanner onto the hexagon to make sure you have the right one. Be careful you do not try using a spanner of the wrong system. It may go onto the hexagon but be such a sloppy fit that as soon as you apply pressure the corners of the hexagon shear off and then not even the correct spanner will work properly.

Types of spanner

Open end flat

This is the simplest spanner and very widely used. Sometimes only single ended but in general double ended, with two consecutive sizes on the two ends. The jaws are offset at an

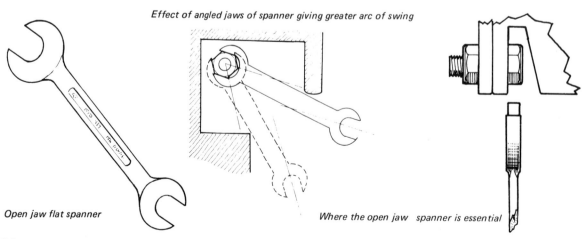

Effect of angled jaws of spanner giving greater arc of swing

Open jaw flat spanner

Where the open jaw spanner is essential

angle from the line of the handle, which is very useful where only a limited movement of the spanner is available. By repeatedly turning the spanner over, the arc of movement can be increased by up to twice the offset angle.

The open jaw spanner is a necessity in situations where there is very little axial clearance. Flat spanners are available individually or in sets covering a complete range of sizes. In a set there may be one end for each size, or alternatively each size may appear twice, once as the big end of the spanner and once as the smaller end. The latter arrangement can be useful when faced with the common situation of requiring two spanners simultaneously of the same size, one for the bolt head and one for the nut.

Ring

On these spanners the open jaws are replaced by a closed ring which has twelve notches on the inside corresponding to the corners of two hexagons offset by 30 degrees. This type of spanner can be much slimmer, without risk of failure, and can therefore be used in situations where the nut or bolt head is closely surrounded by obstructions. The ability to locate at 30 degree intervals also allows use with a more restricted arc of swing. To make the tool even more useful for getting into awkward corners, some ring spanners have the ring offset axially from the handle. Sometimes a ring spanner will be combined with the same size flat spanner. The ring spanner will not slip off easily once it is correctly fitted onto the hexagon and considerable pressure can be applied to the end of the spanner with greater safety than with an open-ended one. However a minimum axial clearance is needed to get the spanner onto the hexagon and this is sometimes not available.

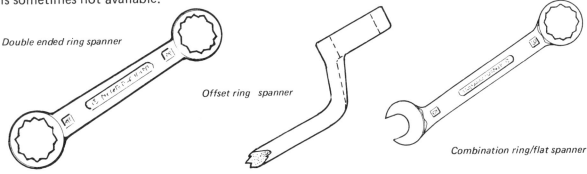

Double ended ring spanner

Offset ring spanner

Combination ring/flat spanner

Box

A steel tube which has been hammered into a hexagon shape at each end; one smaller than the tube and the other larger. The body of the tube is pierced with at least two pairs of holes. Through these holes a steel bar (the 'tommy' bar) is passed which can then be used to rotate the spanner. The box spanner is necessary for dealing with fastenings which are recessed and cannot

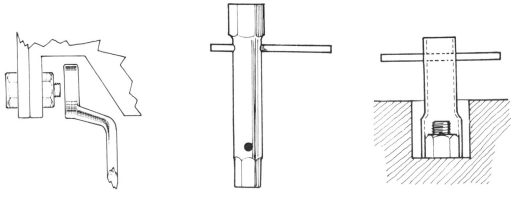

Space needed to fit a ring spanner   *Box spanner with tommy bar*   *Recessed nut that needs box spanner*

be reached with other spanners. Spark plugs are common examples of this problem. In general, the box spanner is not very strong and it is difficult to get adequate pressure on larger screws.

Socket

The socket spanner is a development of the ring spanner and the box spanner. The working part of the spanner is a steel forging, a tube, with a hollow on one end cut internally with the same toothed pattern as a ring spanner, and designed to drop over a nut or bolt head. On the opposite end is a square socket into which can be fitted the driving components, which can be one of a variety.

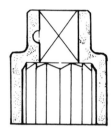

Socket spanner

The simplest is a square driving shaft with a sliding tommy bar through it. Extension shafts can be 'socketed' in between the handle and the working head. The square spigot usually has a spring loaded ball set in its side to retain the socket. A very useful type of handle is the ratchet

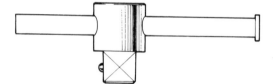 

Tommy bar drive for socket   *Extension shaft for socket drive*

drive. In this the driving square spigot can rotate inside the end of a handle. A ratchet can be set to transmit the drive to the square spigot by movement of the handle in any direction. This type of drive allows very fast tightening and untightening even when the space for movement is restricted. A 'brace' type of driving handle is also available.

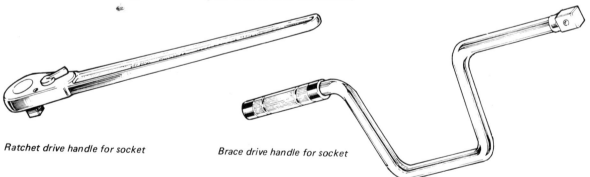

Ratchet drive handle for socket   *Brace drive handle for socket*

Although the components are obtainable separately, most people tend to start off by buying a complete boxed set which usually contains at least two alternative handles, an extension shaft and a consecutive range of socket heads. The most common kits have ½ inch drive squares; the 3/8 inch square gives compact tools more suitable for automobile use.

The socket spanner is a very versatile tool but has the ring spanner's requirement for a minimum axial clearance and will also not normally allow much protrusion through a nut because of the shallowness of the closed socket. Special deep sockets can be obtained and one type you may find useful is a special one made for handling spark plugs. It has an internal rubber collar

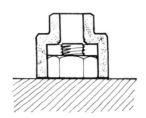

Limitation of depth of standard socket

Special deep socket for sparking plugs

which avoids the risk of breaking the plug insulator, and holds the plug to ease extraction. Cranked extensions are available to ease area of working.

Adjustable

To provide the correct spanner for every job is an ideal which is not usually achieved by the do-it-yourselfer. You will probably therefore provide yourself with an assortment of spanners matched to your most common needs and back up this set with one or more adjustable spanners. These are always parallel open jaw spanners and they come in two main types. In the one type the opening of the jaws is at right angles to the line of the handle (often known as a King Dick). A fixed jaw at one end is matched by a sliding jaw which can be moved over quite a wide range by a knurled nut which acts on a screw attached to the movable jaw.

In the second type the jaws face the direction normal with flat spanners, slightly offset from the line of the handle (parrot jaw). The moving jaw in this type has a much more limited range and is moved by rotating a knurled worm wheel which engages in teeth cut in the base of the moving jaw. This type of adjustable spanner is generally made from high tensile alloy steels and is slimmer and stronger than the first type but has a more restricted range of adjustment.

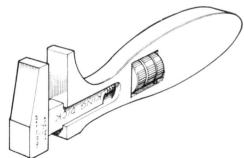

'King Dick' type of adjustable spanner

'Parrot jaw' type of adjustable spanner

Special spanners

Allen keys

These are used with hexagon socket head screws. They simply consist of pieces of high tensile steel hexagon bar with a right-angle bend. One end or the other is fitted into the socket in the screw and then used as a lever to rotate the screw. They come in a range of consecutive sizes to match the screw sizes/threads and can be obtained separately or in sets. A set of Allen keys is usually supplied with the long arm of each key pushed into a simple spiral spring clip which is attached to a ring.

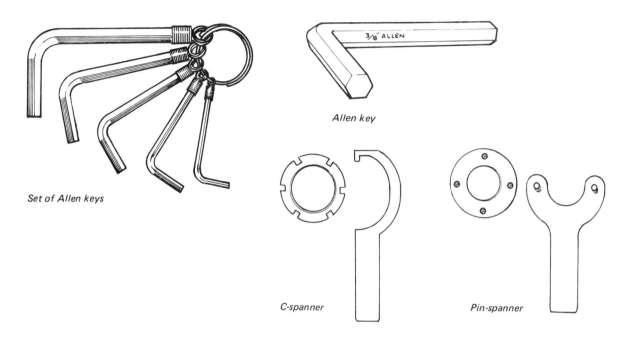

Set of Allen keys

Allen key

C-spanner

Pin-spanner

C-spanners

Sometimes a large diameter threaded collar is required on a shaft where there is a very limited axial space. For applying leverage to such a collar the C-spanner is often used. The hook on one end fits into a notch in the collar and the spanner then fits around it. These spanners are usually made to fit a particular requirement.

Pin-spanners

Another means of dealing with the same large diameter screw problem where the face of the collar is accessible. Pairs of diametrically opposite holes are drilled in the collar. The spanner has pins protruding from its face which match these holes. Like the C-spanner, the pin-spanner is usually made to fit a particular job.

Torque spanners

In many engineering situations (such as tightening up bearings) it is important that a screw is tightened up to exert a particular force (within a tolerance). This force is related by formulae to the rotational force (or torque) needed on each nut or screw. This force is expressed either in terms of pounds/feet or kilogram/centimetres. In either case it is the product of a force and the length of the spanner on which it is applied. For example, if a specification requires a torque of 15 pounds/feet on a particular nut and your spanner to fit that nut is 18 inches long, you can achieve the desired result by attaching a spring balance to the end of the spanner and pulling until you register a load of 10 pounds. (10 pounds x 1½ feet = 15 pounds/feet.)

Load indicating torque spanner

Preset release torque spanner

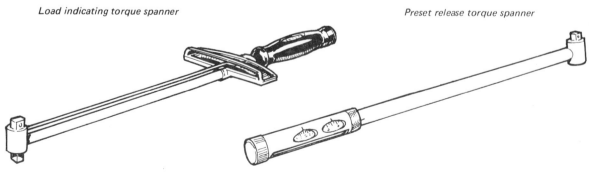

This method is not, however, likely to be very satisfactory if you are working in a restricted space; a 'torque spanner' which provides the necessary measuring facilities is the tool to use. These always have a square spigot to take standard socket spanners and extensions so you need only one torque handle for all sizes of socket. They come in two types. In one case you get a continuous reading of the load you are applying. The other type has some form of setting dial on which you preset the load you wish to apply. When this load is reached a latch is released and you cannot apply any more pressure until the mechanism is reset.

Use of spanners

It might seem obvious — you just fit the spanner on and then pull or push. Well, yes, that **is** the general idea but there are a number of points about the way you do it which are helpful.

For a start, even before you pick up the spanner, make sure the nut or bolt head is clean. If it has been painted you may have difficulty in getting the correct spanner to fit on. Make sure that the threads screw freely; a drop of oil helps and will reduce the risk of future corrosion. If a nut is very tight, take it off again and have a look at the threads; perhaps the nut or screw threads have been damaged. It is particularly important for a nut or screw to be free running if a torque spanner is to be used. If there is excessive friction it can invalidate the torque measurement.

With fine threads it is easy to get a nut 'cross-threaded'; in this state the threads on one side are one thread lower than on the other side. If you force a nut on in this state you will strip the threads completely. The technique for correctly starting a nut is to place it on the end of the bolt and rotate it backwards while gently pressing towards the bolt. As the ends of the two threads pass each other, the nut will drop towards the bolt by the thickness of one thread. This 'click' is quite noticeable, and if rotation forward is then started the threads will mesh correctly without any problem.

Make sure your spanner fits the hexagon correctly. It should just slide on with only the very slightest free movement. If you can move the spanner relative to the hexagon by more than about 10 degrees you have either got the wrong spanner or, in the case of an open jaw spanner, one which has been overstrained and sprung the jaws. When using an adjustable spanner it is particularly important to get the jaws closed right up to the hexagon. You will often find a tendency for the jaws to slacken off gradually with repeated applications, so don't forget to reset regularly, particularly before you apply the final pressure.

Whenever possible use two hands; one to steady the working end of the spanner on the hexagon while the other applies the force. Before you apply full force on a spanner, make sure

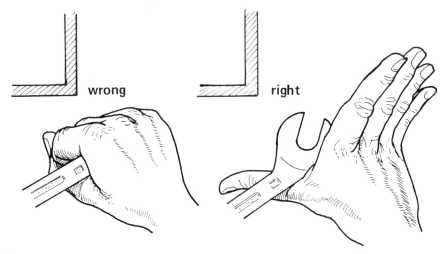

wrong   right

Guard your knuckles

you are in a secure position. The spanner might slip, the bolt might break or it may simply come undone unexpectedly, but in any case you will be suddenly left with your effort unopposed.

If you have a choice, always pull the spanner towards you; you will generally have more control this way. If you must push away from yourself, avoid doing it with your hand closed around the spanner. Use the flat of your palm, then if the spanner slips, your knuckles will not hit that sharp edge which is always just in the way. If you are working in a very restricted space with a smaller spanner, try to use the muscles of your hands rather than your arms to apply the pressure. This can often be done by hooking your fingers around a nearby projection as well as the spanner and then squeezing. This method allows a smoother, more controlled pressure to be applied.

Double ended spanners are usually proportioned so that a normal strength person can apply sufficient force to pull up tight a steel nut and bolt of the large-end size. This means that the small-end size bolt can be overloaded as can one made of a weaker material than steel, say, brass. When tightening, apply a steady force; jerking can apply stresses many times that of a steady pull. Never use a hammer on a spanner when tightening, although it may be necessary when undoing a badly corroded fastening. If you must, use a soft face mallet to protect your spanner.

When unscrewing old fastenings, or using anti-vibration nuts, you may find that you need to hold both bolt and nut at the same time. If you haven't got enough hands for this, or have only one spanner of the correct size, you can sometimes achieve the result with a wedge. If one of the hexagons is close to another surface, a screwdriver blade or other suitable wedge pushed between in the direction of rotation can often hold the bolt head securely enough.

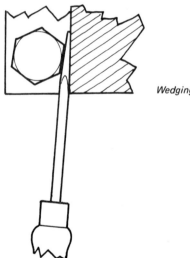

Wedging a bolt head to stop it turning

The basic tool for non-hexagon head screws is the engineer's screwdriver. These come in two general types — the traditional flat blade and the Phillips or Posidriv cross blade, with a variety of blade widths and thicknesses, and shaft lengths.

Use the thickest and widest blade that will fit the screw. Small blades will twist and damage the slot in the screw head. Use a longer screwdriver if you have any choice, as it allows you to apply a greater force to a screw. The tip of the blade should be slightly curved inwards — hollow ground (see diagram). If it is curved outwards it will not properly fit the slot in the screw head. A flat blade screwdriver should be flat and square across the tip; if it is curved the blade will not act

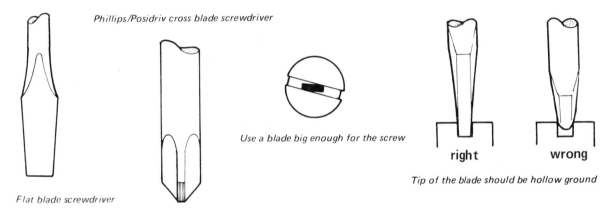

Phillips/Posidriv cross blade screwdriver

Use a blade big enough for the screw

right   wrong

Tip of the blade should be hollow ground

Flat blade screwdriver

over the full area of the screw slot and may damage the screw. If you have to re-sharpen a screwdriver, be careful not to overheat it with grinding. This can soften the metal and make the tool useless. Use a file for sharpening, it is safer.

The simple screwdriver has a plain handle secured onto the shaft. Wooden handles tend to get chipped and splintered in a tool box and absorb oil, so pick ones with moulded plastic handles.

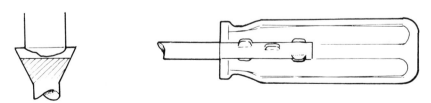

Blade should be square across the end

Use plastic handled screwdrivers

There are also two types of ratchet drive screwdrivers. These speed up running a screw in or out because you do not have to relocate the blade or your hand after each twist; the handle simply slides over the ratchet on the return movement. The simpler of these types has just a ratchet drive which can be set either for clockwise or anticlockwise action or locked.

out of action. The more complicated type, usually called a 'pump-ratchet' screwdriver, has an additional feature. When a catch is released, a telescopic portion of the handle is pushed out by a spring. This telescopic slide has a spiral groove on its outside so that if pressure is applied to the handle to force the slide back in it rotates the screwdriver blade at the end. With this tool a few quick 'pumps' on the handle can spin a screw into or out of position very quickly, just leaving the final pressure to be applied by normal hand rotation.

Always clean out the slot in a screw before using a screwdriver. Accumulated dirt or paint will stop the blade entering properly and will probably result in the edges of the slot being torn off as the blade twists out. If a straight slot type screw head has been damaged it is sometimes possible to recut the slot enough with a fine hacksaw to allow its extraction. A screw with a damaged slot should not of course ever be re-used.

Countersunk head screws are particularly prone to sticking when they have been done up tightly. Placing the screwdriver in the slot and giving it a sharp blow on the end with a hammer can often loosen a stubborn one. Another technique is to get extra leverage by clamping the screwdriver shaft with a 'Mole-grip' (see Chapter 15) and using both hands. Make sure the blade is well secured in the screw before trying this trick.

Screws used in thin sheet metal can very easily be cross-threaded. Don't force them in; you will just strip the thread completely. Screws threaded into plastic mouldings, particularly self-tapping screws wear the material each time they are taken in and out. Care should be taken not to overtighten them as this can finally rip out an already weakened thread.

Smaller screws in awkward spots can be handled conveniently with a spring loaded device which slides onto a screwdriver and holds the screw onto the tip of the blade.

Ratchet screwdriver

For getting small screws into awkward places

The preceding few chapters have been concerned with devices for fastening things together. In many cases the joint between these components must act as a seal to contain, or exclude, liquids or gases. In high precision engineering it is possible to produce a near perfect seal between metal components. The standard of finish required to achieve this is however impracticable in the majority of engineering devices you are likely to encounter. There have, therefore, been evolved a number of techniques which serve to compensate the inaccuracies in normal commercial work and allow tightly sealed joints to be regularly made.

Plain face joint

In this type two flat metal surfaces are held together under pressure, usually by nuts and bolts, to form the joint to be sealed. A basic requirement is that the faces should be flat and smooth, but the larger and more heavily stressed the components, the more difficult it is to avoid distortion in service. So, you will find almost invariably a 'gasket' interposed between the two faces. A gasket is a piece of thin material which will compress enough to follow the irregularities of the joint surfaces. It is normally cut to cover the whole of the surface of the joint faces and has holes in it to allow the passage of the fastening bolts. A variety of different materials are used in automobiles, each selected to meet a particular need. Some of the more common applications are listed here.

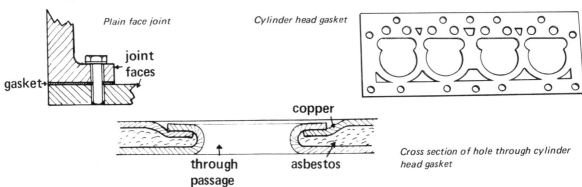

Metal/Asbestos

The main use of this material is for the very large joint between the cylinder head and cylinder block of the engine. It consists of a sandwich of asbestos between two layers of metal, usually copper. It can withstand very high temperatures and pressures, can compensate for distortions over large surfaces, and yet is dimensionally stable over a long time. Cylinder head gaskets are complex, and fairly expensive, components. Openings have to be provided to accurately locate not only with the cylinder bores but also all the cooling water passages, lubricating oil passages, valve operation passages, fixing bolts, etc which make a cylinder head more holey than a Gruyere cheese! The asbestos filling is porous and all the holes, except for those which fit over bolts, are sealed by the two layers of metal being rolled together.

Asbestos

A fairly hard gasket material, usually compounded with graphite, which is used for other high temperature joints, such as exhaust manifolds.

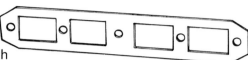
Exhaust manifold gasket

Cork

Sometimes used alone and sometimes compounded with a rubbery type of substance, cork is frequently used for sealing joints against oil. For example, sump, valve cover and gearbox joints.

Rubber/Neoprene

Used as a general purpose gasket material for smaller, lower temperature joints, particularly where there may be large errors in the joint faces. For example, in the weather sealing of bodywork.

Fibre/Paper

Thin layers of a hard red fibre or a type of paper will be found in places where the accuracy of the joint is good and only a slight resilience is needed. Often used on carburettors and other joints exposed to petrol.

Gasket compounds

A variety of semi-liquid and plastic compounds are available which can be used to create a seal if a preformed gasket is not available.

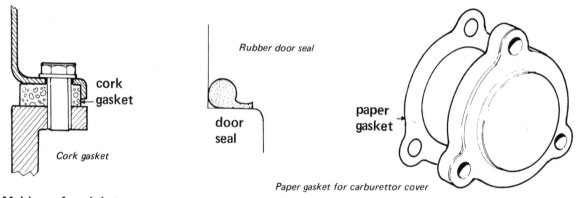

cork gasket

Cork gasket

Rubber door seal

door seal

paper gasket

Paper gasket for carburettor cover

Making a face joint

Only in an emergency should a metal/asbestos gasket be used more than once. Other types should be examined with care and re-used only if they still appear to be resilient. Cork and rubber gaskets are particularly likely to deteriorate.

Make sure that the joint faces are clean and flat, paying particular attention to fragments of an old gasket which may be left. Make sure there are no burrs around holes or at the edges of the joint face. Make sure that **all** the holes in a new gasket line up and you have it on the right way up. It is not uncommon to find that a gasket is symmetrical with the exception of, say, one hole. If will fit on upside down, but the odd hole will be blocked and it might be vital. When replacing an old gasket, make sure that it goes back in the original position even if it quite safely could be fitted another way. It will have been moulded to the roughness of the joint and is more likely to seal well if replaced in the same position.

A smear of grease over both faces of the joint before assembly will aid the final seal. More sophisticated jointing compounds can be obtained but in general should not be needed, although they can salvage a distorted joint which otherwise might have to be scrapped.

When tightening down the fastenings of a flat face joint, it is important to maintain a uniform pressure to avoid distorting the joint. This is particularly important on large joints

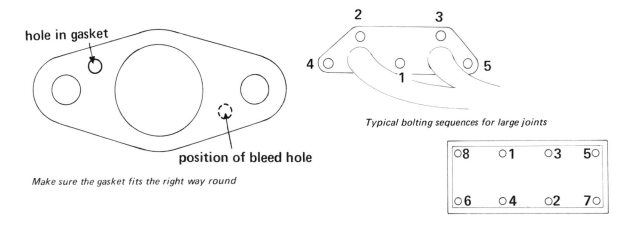

hole in gasket

position of bleed hole

Make sure the gasket fits the right way round

Typical bolting sequences for large joints

requiring high pressure, such as for a cylinder head or exhaust manifold. First tighten down the nuts or bolts all around until they are just finger tight. Then take up equal amounts on bolts on opposite sides, moving around in a sequence of the type shown in the diagram. As you increase the pressure, each successive cycle should be a progressively smaller movement. First a full turn say, then half a turn, then a quarter turn, and so on. Most vehicle manuals give a specific tightening sequence for the cylinder head joint. Be careful when tightening up aluminium joints as they are very easily distorted by uneven tightening.

Metal pipe joints
Flared end

In this type of joint, the resilience needed to give a good seal is achieved in the tube wall itself. The end of the tube is rolled with a special tool to a flared or tapered shape. The component against which the sealed joint has to be made then has a tapered boss which fits into the tube flare and a screwed collar which fits outside the flare. The action of tightening up the screwed collar forces the tapered boss into the end of the pipe which is squeezed between the two taper surfaces. Preparation of a pipe for this type of joint requires special tools, and if you require, say, a replacement brake pipe, it is safest to take the old pipe or a wire template to a specialist dealer. He will cut the pipe to length, bend to the shape you want and form the flared ends, for a small sum. Remember, the screwed collar must be slid onto the pipe **before** the flare is formed.

Flared end pipe joint

'Olive joint'

This type of joint gets its name from one of the components which in smaller sizes is reminiscent in shape of a stuffed olive. Like the flared pipe end joint, this type relies on the wedging action of two conical surfaces. In this case the taper is on the fitting and on a separate metal sleeve, the 'olive' which just slips over the pipe. As the threaded collar of the fitting is tightened up, not only does the tapered face of the olive form a seal with the component, but the relatively soft olive is compressed to form a seal onto the pipe. There are many patent variations on this basic design, with single and double tapered olives and ones with internal cutting edges. In most cases, once the joint has been tightened up the olive has been squeezed so tightly onto the pipe that it is not subsequently removable even when the joint is undone.

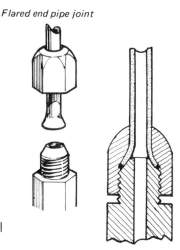

Section through flared joint showing sealing faces (exaggerated)

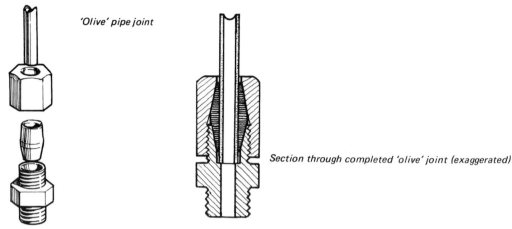

'Olive' pipe joint

Section through completed 'olive' joint (exaggerated)

Flange

A type of joint found on larger diameter pipes. A circular, triangular or square 'flange', a thick plate of metal with a hole in the centre, is attached to the end of the pipe in a permanent manner, such as by welding. This provides a flat face at right angles to the centre line of the pipe and this is now treated as a face joint, usually with a gasket.

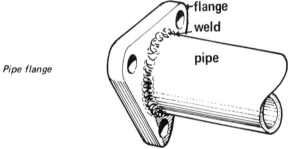

flange
weld
pipe

Pipe flange

'Banjo' joint

Like the flange, this is a fitting permanently attached to the end of a smaller diameter pipe which creates a flat face joint. In this case there are two sealing faces available which are parallel to the centre line of the pipe. Normally a special screw is used to locate and tighten up the face joint. This screw is often hollow with the flow of liquid or gas passing through it. The 'banjo' joint is often to be found on petrol pipe lines.

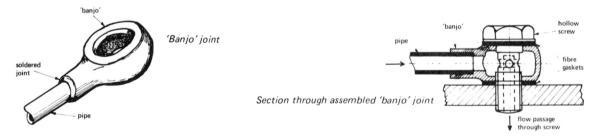

'banjo'

'Banjo' joint

soldered joint

pipe

'banjo'

pipe

hollow screw

fibre gaskets

Section through assembled 'banjo' joint

flow passage through screw

Flexible hose joints

Push fit

The simplest hose joint of all relies on the elasticity of the tubing itself, which is pushed over a spigot slightly larger than the internal diameter of the hose. Sometimes the spigot will be corrugated to give a better grip and seal. This type of joint will often be found on petrol and vacuum connections for carburettors and on windscreen washers. It is not capable of withstanding much pressure. Sometimes a spring wire clip will be added to give added security.

Wire clip

To provide security against higher internal pressures, especially on larger diameter hoses, such as for cooling circuits, it is usual to add some form of external clamp. The cheapest type (and therefore most often used on automobiles!) is made from strong steel wire with a screw and nut device for tightening the clip around the hose. The pipes, onto which hoses with this type of clip fit, are either plain or have a ridge formed at the end to help retain the hose.

Worm-drive clip

This type of hose clamp is more commonly known by the trade name of one make, the 'Jubilee Clip'. It consists of a flat strip of metal which can be wrapped around the hose. Permanently attached to one end of the strip is a casing which contains a 'worm' or screw which can be turned by a screwdriver. The free end of the metal strip is cut with oblique notches which match the pitch of the worm. When the clip is wrapped around the hose, the free end is tucked into a slot underneath the worm which is then rotated with a screwdriver. The threads of the worm engage in the notches in the strip and pull it through, thereby tightening up the clip. This type of clip is reliable, can exert very considerable pressure without cutting through a rubber hose, but is rather expensive.

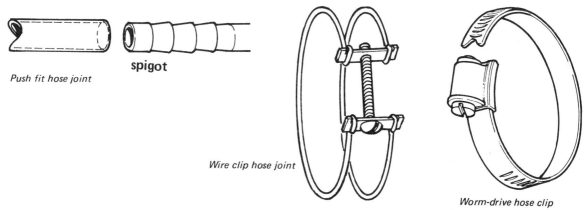

spigot

Push fit hose joint

Wire clip hose joint

Worm-drive hose clip

Brake hose joints

A special type of high pressure joint is used on hydraulic brake hose pipes. These need special tools and testing facilities to assemble them to the hosepipe and you should never attempt to interfere with them. The removable part of the joint is usually a conical metal (male end) to metal seating (female end) similar to the metal pipe joints discussed earlier. Replacement brake hoses are always purchased complete with the joint fittings already attached.

Assembling hose joints

Make sure that the correct hose diameter is being used. It should just be a tight push fit onto the spigot. Too tight and the hose may split in service; too loose and it will not be possible to get

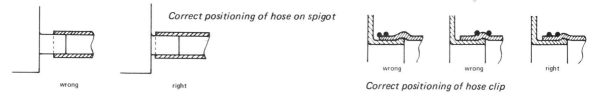

Correct positioning of hose on spigot

wrong   right

Correct positioning of hose clip

wrong   wrong   right

a reliable seal. Wetting the inside of the hose end can make it easier to push onto the spigot, particularly if there is a lip to go over. Make sure there is no twist in the hose before clamping in position, and push it right onto the spigot. If a hose clip is being used, it will usually be found to be easier to connect the two ends of the clip together and slide it onto the hose first, rather than spring the clip around after the hose is on the spigot. A hose clip should be screwed up tight, but be careful with the wire type as they can cut right into some soft hose materials. Make sure that the clip is well onto the hose but is still enclosing the pipe spigot (see diagram).

Exhaust pipe joints

This special class of pipe joints is characterised by being able to stand very rapid fluctuations in temperature, operation at very high temperatures and rapid corrosion. There are usually two different types of joint involved in an exhaust pipe. The first is the joint between the pipe and the exhaust manifold at the engine. On older engines this was usually a flanged face joint with a metal/asbestos or asbestos gasket. On more modern machinery it tends to be a flared end joint with the flared pipe end held against a conical seating on the manifold by a bolted collar. Whatever the type of joint, this is the one to pay attention to first. It is subjected to very hot gases at high pressure, and leakages at this joint can easily result in poisonous carbon-monoxide entering the inside of the vehicle. This is one place where you really have to get it bolted up tightly.

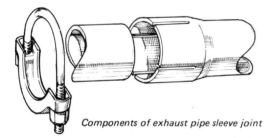

Components of exhaust pipe sleeve joint

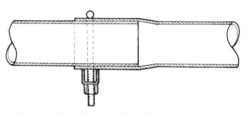

Cross section of assembled exhaust pipe joint

The second type of joint is used between the various sections of pipe and the silencer(s). It is usually a simple overlapped sleeve joint. The end of one pipe is rolled out until its diameter is sufficient to just slide over the end of the other. The larger pipe is slit lengthwise in two or more places to give some resilience. After the two pipes are pushed together a clamp is placed around the outside to squeeze together the split end of the outer tube. Deburr the ends of both pipes before attempting to assemble them and coat the mating surfaces with a high temperature jointing compound (Gun-gum can be quite good for this). When the two halves of the joint have been telescoped together, hammer the outside tube to close it in; do not just rely on the clamp. Only when the joint is already quite tight, fit the clamp and tighten it well up.

A graphite lubricant for all nuts on exhaust systems will make later unscrewing easier.

We have discussed the main methods of fastening components together in such a manner that they can be readily taken apart again. Before leaving this subject of 'demountable' fastenings, we should look briefly at pins and spring clips as a type of fastener which you will find used in automobiles. We will then look at the permanent methods of fastening components together. Your prime interest in these will be concerned with possible repairs.

Split pins

The split pin is made from steel with a semi-circular cross section. A length of this material is folded back on itself so that where the two legs lie together, they form a cylindrical pin. The bend is formed as an open eye and the two legs are not the same length. The split pin is used generally as a retainer to keep together two or more components which are interlocked but might work loose. In general the split pin is not expected to take much load. It is very commonly used, where a component fits onto a shaft, to stop the component sliding off. A hole is drilled through the shaft, the component is slid on past the hole, and a split pin is dropped into the hole. The eye at one end stops it going right through and the legs are bent around the shaft at the other end to stop the pin coming out. The difference in length of the legs makes it easier to separate them. Preferably split pins should not be re-used at all after having been straightened out, and certainly not more than twice.

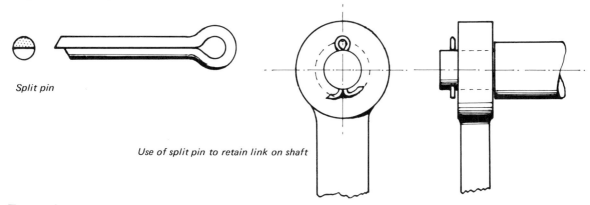

Split pin

Use of split pin to retain link on shaft

Taper pins

Where the pin is required to take a significant load, the split pin is too weak and a solid pin must be used. Occasionally this will be a parallel pin which is itself retained by, perhaps, split pins. More commonly a taper pin will be used. This is round in section and has a uniform small taper along its length. The angle of the taper is critical and is chosen so that the pin will wedge tightly in its hole. If you have to dismantle a taper-pinned component, check carefully which is the small end — it is not easy to see. A sharp blow with a hammer on the small end will free the pin — hitting the other end gets you nowhere! Make sure that when you reassemble the component it goes back in exactly the same position and that you insert the pin from the correct side as the hole will normally have been reamed with a taper.

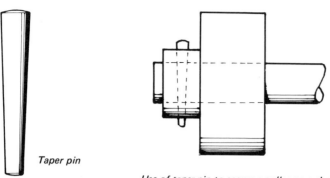

Taper pin

Use of taper pin to secure a collar on a shaft

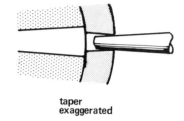

taper
exaggerated

The problem of re-assembling taper
pinned components

Cotter-pins

This nomenclature is sometimes loosely used to refer to split-pins, but the cotter-pin is a completely different device. It is sometimes used to fix a component to a shaft so that they must rotate together (it is an alternative to the taper pin for this purpose). The cotter-pin consists of a parallel round pin with a tapering flat cut on one side and a threaded portion at one end. The shaft will have a corresponding flat cut on it. The cotter-pin is passed through a hole in the component to be fixed, so that the flat on the pin rests against the flat on the shaft. Tightening a nut on the threaded end of the pin wedges the component, shaft and pin tightly together.

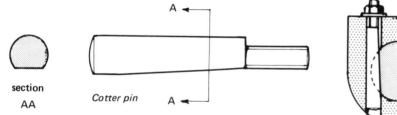

section
AA

Cotter pin   A

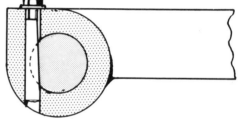

Use of cotter pin to secure a lever to a shaft

Cotters

Although not a pin fastening at all, the cotter also relies on a wedging action. This device is regularly used for securing valve springs to the valve stems. It is best described as a steel sleeve with a parallel cylindrical bore and a tapered, conical exterior, which has been split longitudinally into two halves. When used with a valve spring, the spring is placed over the valve stem with a fitting at the free end which has an internal taper matching the cotter. The spring is compressed and the two halves of the split cotter are placed around the valve stem, fitting into a groove. A dab of stiff grease will hold them in place while the spring is released. The collar at the end of the spring then squeezes the cotter together and locks the spring to the valve stem.

A pair of taper cotters

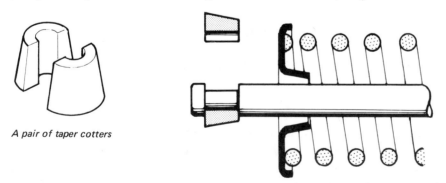

Cotters used to secure a valve stem to its spring

Circlips

It is sometimes required to locate a component on a shaft or in a recess so that it is free to rotate but not to move axially. Common examples are oil seals and bearings. A very neat device for this purpose is the circlip. It consists of an accurately made spring steel ring which is not quite a complete circle, with a small perforated 'ear' at each end of the spring. To use a circlip on a shaft, a small groove wide enough to take the thickness of the circlip and about half its depth is machined at the appropriate place on the shaft. By pulling the 'ears' of the circlip apart, it can be opened far enough to slide onto the shaft. When the groove is reached, the circlip drops in and forms a secure barrier preventing anything moving along the shaft past it. To remove the circlip, the 'ears' must again be pulled apart far enough to spring it out of its groove. Special pliers with

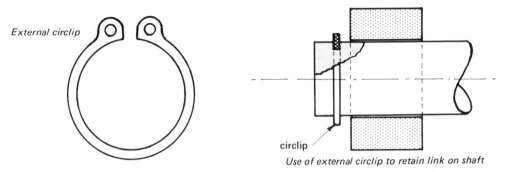

External circlip

circlip

Use of external circlip to retain link on shaft

pointed tips which fit the holes in the 'ears' can be obtained, but for occasional use a pair of small screwdrivers used as levers will probably meet your needs. So far the 'outside' circlip has been described; there is also the 'inside' circlip, with the ears pointing inward, which is used for locating in grooves machined in a hole instead of on a shaft.

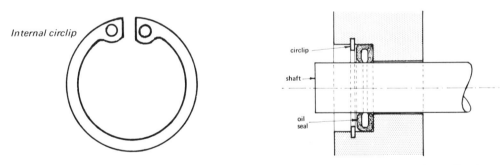

Internal circlip

circlip

shaft

oil seal

Use of internal circlip to retain an oil seal

Spring clips

Scattered throughout the modern automobile will be found an enormous variety of spring clips used for attaching decorative trim, wiring, carpets, etc. In general they tend to be small pieces of spring steel with one part designed to locate in a hole or on the edge of the supporting material and the remainder of the clip designed to locate the material to be secured. Much of the decorative trim in automobiles has hidden fastenings of this type. If you believe that a particular piece of trim should be removable, perhaps because it would be the only way to gain access to some mechanism, examine it carefully for fastenings. If there are no obvious screw heads or similar signs, it is probably held by spring clips and a bit of gentle levering with a screwdriver should release it.

Welding

In Chapter 3 it was pointed out that steel is the basic material used in most automobiles.

Welding is the basic means of permanently fastening together steel components. In the welding process the metal is heated up until the edges which are to be joined together actually melt and the two pieces fuse together. When cold, a correctly made weld should be as strong as the original material. The heat is applied by the use of a high temperature gas flame (oxy/acetylene or oxy/propane welding), by the heat from an electric spark produced between the metal to be welded and a special electrode (arc welding), or by passing a very heavy electric current between the two components to be joined (resistance welding). None of these processes are for the amateur. If you have bent your tin-work or want to change its shape, you will have to hire the services of a specialist at your local garage or engineering workshop.

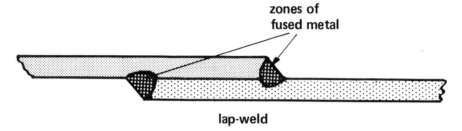

zones of
fused metal

lap-weld

Spot-welding

This is a specialised type of welding used extensively in automobile practice. The spot-welding machine clamps the metals to be joined between two water-cooled copper contacts and passes a very heavy electric current through the metal. The current is limited to a small area and heats the metal to melting point in a fraction of a second while at the same time it is being forced together by the pressure of the electrodes. This action forms a localised weld, usually about ¼ inch in diameter. These 'spots' are used to 'stitch' together many of the bodywork panels in modern automobiles. This type of fastening is not nearly as strong as a full weld and will occasionally fail in service. If you have to repair a failed spot weld, or wish to separate and then reassemble spot welded components, it is sometimes quite feasible to drill out the spot and replace it with a rivet (see later).

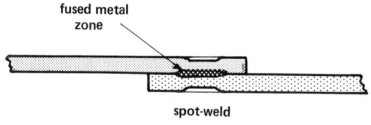

fused metal
zone

spot-weld

Brazing

This process uses lower temperatures than welding. The steel is not raised completely to melting point, but a filling material is used which melts at a lower temperature and will diffuse slightly into the nearly melting steel. Although not as strong as a weld, this process will readily produce joints adequate for normal vehicle repairs, particularly of bodywork. Again it requires skills and equipment not readily available to an amateur, but is sometimes more accessible in a garage than welding.

Soldering

This is a process particularly applicable to non-ferrous metals (copper, brass) where, like brazing, a low melting point metal — solder — is diffused into the surfaces of the metals to be joined. Solder itself is very weak and the essence of a good soldered joint is that it should not rely directly on the strength of the solder to hold it together. Rather, the solder should be used like glue to form the final bond between surfaces already in very close contact.

The most likely place you will need soldering is for electrical connections, where its prime purpose is to ensure a good electrical circuit rather than to take a mechanical load. You might need to use it for emergency repairs to a cooling radiator, but in general the epoxy resin adhesives (see later) are likely to make a better job of most of the traditional uses of solder except the electrical one which is discussed in Chapter 19.

Rivetting

Rivets are used in a similar manner to nuts and bolts but are a relatively permanent fastening. They can be removed only by cutting off the head or drilling them out. The rivet is a cylindrical piece of metal with a head on one end. The parallel portion is passed through holes in the two components to be joined, and then an axial pressure is applied to the rivet. The body of the rivet first swells to fill the hole and then a second head is formed on the other end of the rivet. Rivets come in a great variety of materials and head shapes and can be set either hot or cold.

Snap head rivet

Tubular rivet

For your do-it-yourself workshop you are almost certainly going to be interested only in smaller size, cold set rivets, and lacking proper forming dies you will always end up with flat head rivets. The rivet should be a snug fit in the holes before pressure is applied. For small rivets near the edge of a plate, adequate rivetting pressure can sometimes be applied by pliers or a vice. Usually, however, you will have to rely on a hammer. The rivet head should be backed up by solid metal, preferably resting on the ground or a bench. Failing a solid stop like that, you need something with plenty of inertia. Another hammer is the usual, preferably a sledge hammer if you can get one. Rivetting usually needs the services of someone else as 'holder-up'. Once you have formed a decent head, do not keep on hammering. If the head is too thin the rivet loses strength.

wrong   **right**

Do not hammer a rivet too much

For joining sheet metal, where a larger diameter is needed to avoid tearing, tubular rivets can be used. These require much less force to form the head than the equivalent solid rivet.

For dealing with situations where only one side of the material is accessible, a special type of rivet has been developed. Known as the 'pop-rivet', this is a tubular rivet with a thin stem attached to the non-head end and running through the hollow rivet. The rivet is passed through the hole and a special tool is used to set it. This holds the head of the rivet close against the work and at the same time pulls the stem away from the work. This action causes the formation of a second head on the inaccessible inside end of the rivet. The stem has a constriction near the rivet end, and once sufficient pressure to form the rivet properly has been exceeded, the stem snaps at this constriction (with a sharp 'pop'). A rivet is then left, with a smooth exterior surface, which you know has been formed with the correct pressure. Pop-rivets are available quite cheaply in kits with a hand-setting tool.

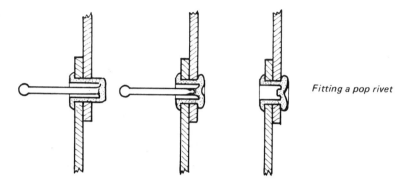

Fitting a pop rivet

Adhesives

Apart from the usual miscellany of minor sticking jobs, there are two particular types of adhesive with which you will need to concern yourself. Automobile manufacturers make considerable use of impact adhesives for attaching interior trim, sound absorption material, carpeting, etc. This type of adhesive is spread on the two components to be joined and can be allowed to dry, becoming just slightly 'tacky'. If these two coated surfaces are now brought together under slight pressure, they will immediately adhere. Sometimes, however, the original coating is not perfect and the components shake loose in service, and you would be wise to use a similar adhesive (such as Evostik) to replace them.

The other important type of adhesive is the epoxy resin group, which while rarely used in manufacture can be invaluable for repairs. The most commonly available one of these adhesives on the do-it-yourself market is 'Araldite'. Like most of the others this is a two component adhesive. Basically, one component is a viscous resin while the other is a liquid 'hardener'. (Sometimes the consistency is changed to suit a particular packaging arrangement.) Kept separate, these components have an indefinite life. As soon as they are mixed, an irreversible chemical reaction starts which will eventually result in a very hard substance.

With the correct proportions of resin and hardener, properly mixed, the resultant adhesive can be used with most materials and can produce joints stronger than the original material in some cases. The 'curing' time is very dependent on temperature. At normal room temperature it takes about 24 hours to develop full strength, but this can be brought down to less than an hour by heating the components above 100°C. For emergency repairs and for many permanent alterations, epoxy resin adhesives can be invaluable.

The Drill

The basic component you will need for making holes is the twist drill, commonly referred to as a 'drill bit'. This is a cylindrical bar of steel having rounded spiral grooves running part of its length and a conical point with cutting edges formed by the termination of the spiral grooves.

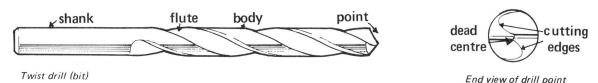

Twist drill (bit)   *End view of drill point*

The cutting edges do not inersect at the point but leave a chisel edge known as the dead centre. The angle of the conical tip is varied according to the material being cut when used by the professional engineer. For your purposes, an included angle at the tip of 120° is a good general shape and would be how the drill is supplied from the factory.

The body of the drill, the fluted part, provides the support and guidance for the cutting edges and defines the finished size of the hole. The flutes allow the chips of cut material to escape from the cutting edge and admit a lubricant if required.

The shank is the part of the drill at the opposite end to the cutting edges, which is gripped by the drilling tool machine which you use. You will be interested only in the straight shank drill, but you need to know that there are taper shank (or Morse taper) drills so that you will not buy one by mistake. These are normally used only in precision machines in factories.

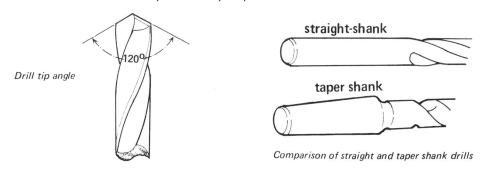

Drill tip angle

Comparison of straight and taper shank drills

Drill size

Drill sizes appear in four different systems — fractional, number, letter and metric sizes.
- the **fractional** size drills range from 1/64 inch to 3½ inches varying in steps of 1/64 inch from one size to the next.
- the **number** size drills range from No 1 measuring 0.228 inch diameter to No 80 which measures 0.0135 inch.
- the **letter** size drills range from A to Z. Letter A is the smallest in the set (0.234 inch) and Z is the largest (0.413 inch).
- the **metric** size drills range from 0.4 mm to 50 mm.

The size quoted is always the overall diameter of the body of the drill, which approximates to the finished size of the hole. Drills can be purchased singly or in complete sets covering a range of sizes. These sets often include a stand or storage rack.

Drill speed

In drilling, the speed of the drill is perhaps the most important factor to be considered. The speed referred to is the surface speed of the cutting edge relative to the material being cut. Clearly, for a given rotational rate a larger diameter drill has a faster cutting speed at the tip than a small drill. So, basic rule number one — for a given material rotate larger drills more slowly than smaller ones. Basic rule number two — the softer the material the faster it should be cut. There is no point in giving the correct speeds as the average do-it-yourself workshop will have little choice, if any.

Marking-out for drilling

The general details of marking-out practice have already been given in Chapter 4, but some points need expansion here. Make sure that the centre mark is big enough to take the dead-centre of the drill. If this is not easily done with the centre punch a pilot hole should be drilled with a small drill first. If a larger hole is to be drilled and its position must be accurate, use the following procedure:

— scribe a circle the finished hole diameter after the centre has been punched.
— scribe another circle a little way inside the first.
— with the centre punch make dimples around the circles to clearly mark the position.
— start the drill and continue cutting until the spot produced by the drill point approaches the inner circle.
— examine this spot for concentricity.
— if it is off centre cut shallow grooves with a chisel on the side towards which the drill must be moved.
— start the drill again and it will be pulled towards the grooves.
— continue this process until the drill is correctly cutting in the centre.

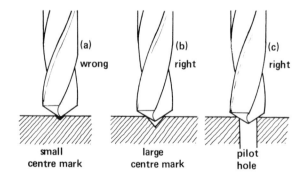

(a) wrong — small centre mark
(b) right — large centre mark
(c) right — pilot hole

Make sure the drill has a good start

Procedure for accurately positioning a larger hole

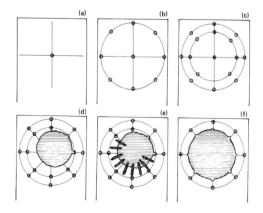

Drilling

Make sure that the drill is properly centred when starting to cut. Concentrate on getting it positioned correctly rather than on getting maximum cutting until the spot is well established. Pressure should then be applied to keep the drill cutting steadily. Too little pressure will cause the drill to just rub without cutting and will give very rapid drill wear. Too much pressure can cause overheating or even make the drill seize up completely.

With hand held drilling tools it is always wise to drill a pilot hole if the final hole diameter is above 0.3 inch. Partly, this is to give better guidance and partly to ease the cutting load by taking more than one cut.

The work being drilled must be securely held. Be extremely careful if the piece you are drilling is held by one hand. As the drill breaks through it may jam and twist the work out of your hand and whirl it around. Its a well know technique for losing fingers!

Be careful when drilling thin material as there is a tendency for the first flute which passes right through to pull the drill to one side and then to feed the whole drill through without cutting a hole out to size. This problem can be eased by reducing the cutting pressure as the drill starts to break through. A better solution is to back up the thin material with a hard-wood block clamped up tightly and then drill through into the wood.

If you are drilling a blind hole (that is one which does not break through the material), put a piece of adhesive tape on the drill to mark the depth of penetration you require.

If you are drilling through a finished surface you will find that the chips being whirled around by the drill can scratch the surface for some way outside the hole. Sticking a piece of transparent tape over the marked out area before you start drilling can avoid this problem.

If you are making heavy cuts or ones which need to be accurate, a lubricant can help to reduce wear and produce a better finished hole.

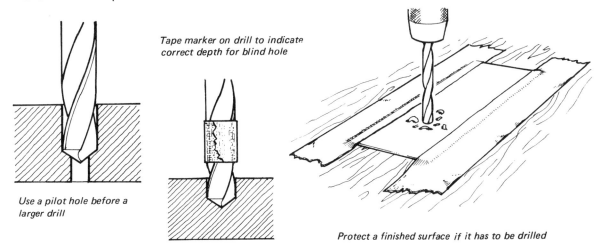

Tape marker on drill to indicate correct depth for blind hole

Use a pilot hole before a larger drill

Protect a finished surface if it has to be drilled

Sharpening

Unless you are doing a great deal of drilling of larger holes, this is not likely to be too much of a problem for you. When a smaller drill eventually becomes blunted it may be more reliable/cheaper to buy a new one than to attempt re-sharpening without the proper fixtures. A worn drill can be seen by an inability to get good shavings coming from the cut, by the blunt feel to the cutting edge, and often by a highly polished area appearing just behind the cutting edge. A small amount of sharpening can be done against a rotating grindstone by being careful to follow the original contours until the cutting edge is restored. This is, however, very difficult to do if repeated sharpening is required, and it is better to try to find a friendly engineering workshop where your drill can be sharpened for you.

Drilling machine

Surprisingly, to use a twist drill effectively you need some means of rotating it. Correctly titled the drilling machine, but often simply referred to as a 'drill', it comes in a variety of forms. The most common these days in the do-it-yourself kit is the general purpose mains electric 'drill'. Not only is this valuable as a basic hand held drilling machine, but with the aid of various attachments can be used for a wide variety of other jobs (polishing, sawing, grinding, turning, etc). If you have a choice, pick a machine with at least two speeds and a chuck able to take up to 3/8 inch diameter drills.

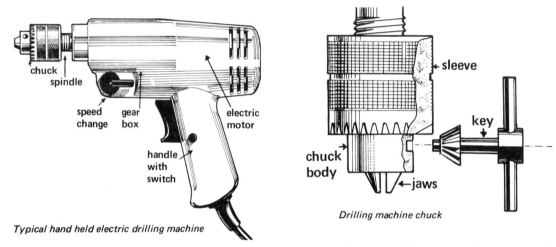

Typical hand held electric drilling machine

Drilling machine chuck

The chuck is the device screwed onto the spindle of the machine which is used to grip the parallel shank of a drill or any shaft which needs to be rotated. On the outside of the chuck is a sleeve which can be rotated relative to the machine spindle. This movement either closes in or opens out a set of, usually three, jaws inside the body of the chuck. To fit a drill the jaws are opened up until the drill shank will drop into the opening between them.

Rotation of the outer sleeve then closes the jaws in until the drill shank is gripped. A loose key with a handle is then inserted into a hole in the side of the chuck and rotated to apply the final gripping pressure on the drill. Do not overstrain the chuck key — you might not get it undone afterwards. But the chuck does need to be locked up tightly. If the drill shank slips when you are cutting hard it will score both drill and chuck jaws, impairing their future accuracy.

It seems so obvious — but many people have started an electric drilling machine with the key still in the chuck. It can cause damage and injury when it flies out. Some manufacturers provide a small spring clip which allows you to secure the chuck key to the mains supply cable. This avoids the problem of remembering where you put it.

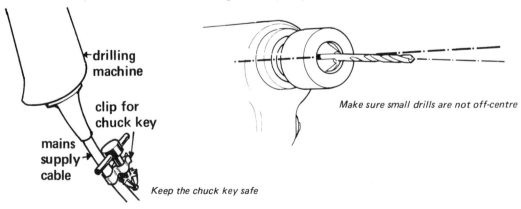

Make sure small drills are not off-centre

Keep the chuck key safe

When putting a small diameter drill into the chuck, watch that it does not drop into the slot between two jaws and become wedged out of centre. If you are using a drill of less than 1/8 inch diameter, it is probably much safer to use a light weight hand 'twist drill' drilling tool. You will have far more control over the drill.

For drilling larger holes in light materials, it is possible to obtain drills with 'turned down' shanks smaller than the diameter of the drill cutting faces. These should be used with caution because although they can fit into the chuck, it is very easy to overload the machine. For use with very large drills, a carpenter's brace will be found useful. It allows the slow speed rotation appropriate to this type of drill.

Cutting large holes

A not uncommon requirement for do-it-yourself car maintenance is the need to cut a largish hole, often of an odd shape, in the thin metal which comprises so much of the modern automobile. Lacking the facilities of large power presses, there are several standard techniques for this operation.

The most common is to drill a line of small holes, nearly touching, around the circumference of the area to be cut out. A sharp chisel is then used to cut through the remaining webs to remove the waste from the centre. This is followed up with a file to remove the ragged remains and take the hole to its finished size.

Of course, if the plate to be cut can be adequately supported, a chisel can be used by itself to take out the hole in one operation, but this is rarely feasible.

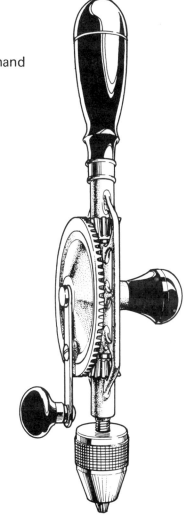

Hand drilling machine

'Turned-down' shank for a drill

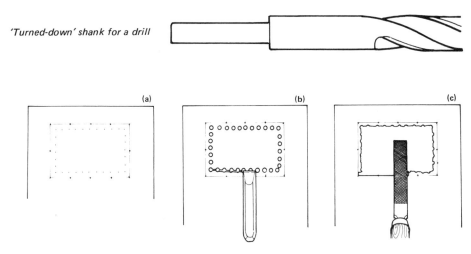

The 'drill and file' method of cutting an aperture

A variant on the 'drill and cut' technique can be used when the area to be cut out has straight edges. In this case a larger hole is cut at each corner and a saw used to cut between them. The hole is again finished to size with a file.

A rotary file can be a useful special tool for such occasions. This is used in a drilling machine like a normal twist drill, but the flutes of the drill are replaced over a large part of its length by file teeth. It can be used by itself for cutting out an odd shape, for increasing the size of a drilled hole or for finishing off a hole roughly cut by one of the other methods.

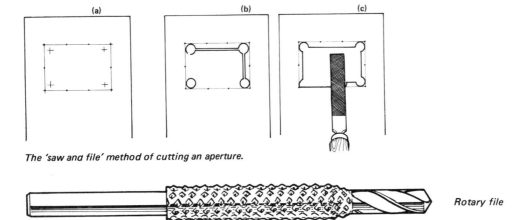

The 'saw ana file' method of cutting an aperture.

Rotary file

Two other special tools which you may encounter, which are useful for cutting larger round holes, are the hole saw (tank cutter) and the hole punch. The hole saw is a carrier to which is fixed a circular blade very similar to a section of a hacksaw blade. They are made in a range of sizes, usually in 1/8 inch steps, and are popular with electricians and pipe-fitters. The hole punch consists of a circular punch and a hollow die coupled by a screw. It is used by drilling a hole through which the screw is passed with the punch on one side of the plate and the die on the other. Tightening the screw causes the punch to shear a clean hole through the plate with very little effort. They are available in 1/8 inch steps up to about 2 inches in diameter, and are commonly used by radio and electronic equipment fitters.

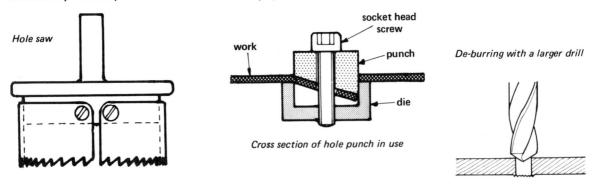

Hole saw

socket head screw

work

punch

die

Cross section of hole punch in use

De-burring with a larger drill

Finishing holes

When a hole has been drilled in metal, 'burrs' or rough edges are left at the entry point and, more noticeably, at the exit point. These should always be removed before the job can be considered to be finished. The simplest way is to take a drill considerably larger than the hole and just rotate it lightly against the burrs. For soft materials this can easily be done by holding the drill in your hand.

If the job requires a very accurately sized hole it must be remembered that the normal twist drill does not provide this. The forces on the cutting edges, misalignment of the drilling tool, vibration and many other factors all introduce errors into the size and positioning of the hole. To obtain accurate sizing, chose a drill 1/64 inch below the desired finished diameter. The hole should then be finished by reaming to size. The reamer has very accurately sized flutes at a much longer spiral than the drill. It has no cutting edges on the end, but the flutes do have cutting edges. If used in the drilling machine, a reamer is normally rotated at about half the speed of the corresponding drill. It is, however, quite common to use a reamer by hand only. If the accurate sizing of the hole is related to aligning components, it is best to pass the reamer through the matching part as well as the hole being reamed. This will ensure that correct alignment is obtained.

Spiral flute reamer

There is a further type of cutting operation closely associated with making holes. This is the production of threads — external ones for studs, bolts or screws, and internal ones into which these components must fit. Although thread cutting is not likely to be a frequent operation, you may be faced with the necessity as part of a repair job. A brief outline of the basic tools and operations is therefore included here for the sake of completeness.

Internal threads

This is perhaps the more likely of the two operations which you might use. The requirement is to transform a plain drilled hole into one which has a perfectly formed thread on the interior surface. The tool used for this operation is the 'tap'. It looks rather like a bolt which has a square end instead of a head. The threads are slightly larger than the normal bolt thread and are very hard. Four deep flutes are cut along the length of the tap and the edges of the threads exposed by these flutes are the cutting tools. Taps are rotated by a simple double handle or 'stock' which fits on the square end. The size of the hole must be slightly smaller than the root diameter of the thread, so it would be impracticable to start the tap cutting if it was parallel all the way. Taps are

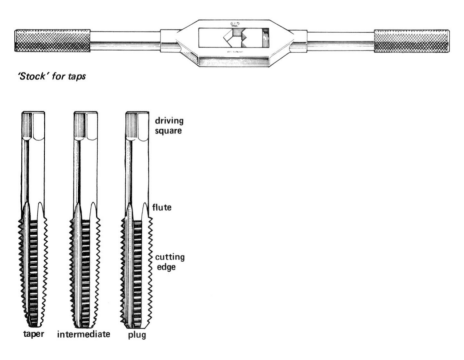

'Stock' for taps

driving
square

flute

cutting
edge

taper   intermediate   plug

Taps for cutting internal threads

therefore given a taper over part of their length and there are three types — taper, intermediate and plug. For the taper tap, only a small proportion is at full diameter and this type is used for the first cut in very tough metals, giving a gradually increasing depth of cut as the tap is screwed in. The intermediate tap is the general purpose tool with a fast taper and a substantial parallel portion. The plug tap is used for 'blind tapped' holes — ones which are not drilled through. The plug has only a very slight lead-in and the threads must first be cut as far as possible with an intermediate tap before taking the cut to the bottom of the hole with the plug tap.

Taps come in the same sizes and thread types as the bolts which are to fit. The correct 'tapping drill' size can be found from standard tables, but in an emergency you can select one by eye to be slightly smaller than the diameter at the root of the thread. Make sure that the tap is started upright and kept perpendicular to the work. Ease the cutting load by unwinding the tap for a couple of turns after every few cutting turns. This backwards rotation cleans out the thread to the finished size and reduces the drag on the tap. A drop of oil or grease will also ease the cutting load. When blind tapping, clean out any chippings from the bottom of the hole before taking the plug tap down the last few turns.

External threading

External threads are cut by a tool — the threading 'die' — which, as you might expect, is the reverse of the tap. The most common form of the die is a circular block of metal with a threaded hole in the centre. Three holes are drilled which break through the thread to form the cutting teeth and additionally the die is slit through to the centre on one side. The die is placed in a holder with handles — the stock. This has three grub screws on one side. The centre one locates in the slit of the die and when tightened up slightly expands the die. This allows the rate of cutting to be adjusted. The other two, when screwed in, locate in indentations in the side of the die and provide the driving force and allow the die to be closed in for a deeper cut.

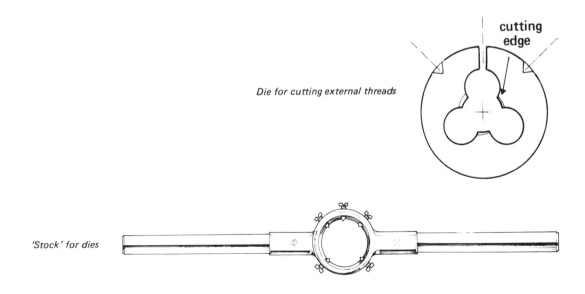

Die for cutting external threads

cutting edge

'Stock' for dies

The size of the plain spindle which is to be threaded should be the same as the overall diameter of the final thread required. The tip should be slightly chamfered to ease the starting of the cut. The die is pressed onto the end of the spindle and rotated, ensuring that it remains at right angles to the spindle. Like the tap, the die should be regularly eased by a backward rotation.

It is also possible to obtain 'die-nuts'. These are similar to standard hexagon nuts with cutting teeth formed internally. They are not adjustable and it is quite tricky to cut a completely new thread with a die-nut alone. They are, however, extremely useful for reconditioning a damaged stud or other threaded component.

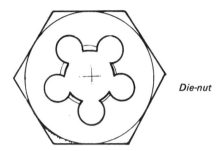

Die-nut

The subject of threaded holes cannot be left without reference to a device known as the 'Helicoil'. A problem particularly common with threaded holes in aluminium castings, or similar soft metals, is what to do if the thread has been overstressed and stripped? In some cases it may be possible simply to drill out the hole and tap it to the next larger size and then fit the appropriately larger screw. However in many cases the configuration of the device being fastened may not allow this to be done and recourse must be had to the Helicoil. This is a spiral of hardened steel wire which has a cross section such that the coil has a correct thread form on both outside and inside. The faulty hole is drilled out and tapped to a size which allows the Helicoil to be screwed into it. The springiness of the coil secures it and the original screw can be fitted.

The basic hacksaw

The engineer's hacksaw is the basic sawing tool you will need. It consists of a frame, usually adjustable to take different length blades, with a pistol grip type of handle at one end. At each end of the frame will be pegs onto which is hooked the cutting blade, one of the pegs being movable to apply tension to the blade.

In choosing your hacksaw look for one with a firm frame, where the handle is positioned so that the lower edge of your hand will be on the line of the blade or below it. This position allows natural thrust of the arm to the blade and gives good control of the direction of cut. The mounting pegs for the blade should be adjustable so that the blade can be faced in any of four ways, and adequate provision should be made for tensioning the blade correctly. This is usually by a wing nut but sometimes some form of lever or cam is used.

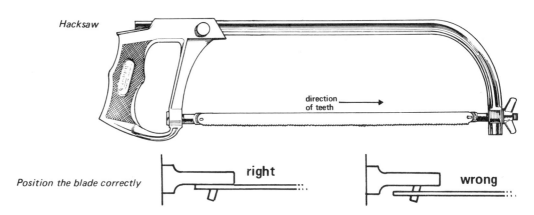

Hacksaw

direction of teeth

Position the blade correctly   **right**   **wrong**

When inserting the blade the teeth should be pointing away from the handle. Before applying tension, make sure that the blade is resting flat against the supporting surfaces and not just hooked on the pegs. The tension applied should be sufficient to hold the blade true when cutting. In use, the blade heats up and expands, and allowance must be made for this loss of tension.

The blade

The hacksaw blade is a series of separate cutting tools on a common carrier. In order to avoid binding in the cut, the teeth must in some way be wider than the back of the blade. This is achieved either by offsetting alternate teeth or by making the blade 'wavy'

Hacksaw teeth

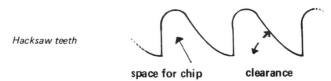

space for chip   clearance

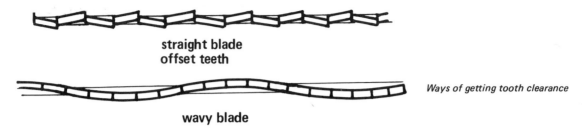

**straight blade
offset teeth**

Ways of getting tooth clearance

wavy blade

Most hacksaw blades are about ½ inch deep, 0.025 inch thick and are available in 10 or 12 inch lengths. Ordinary blades are hardened along the line of the teeth, leaving the back of the blade softer and tougher. Some special blades can be fully hardened or provided with a more flexible spring back.

The tooth spacing is the main point to be considered in the selection of hacksaw blades. Blades are available in a range of tooth pitches from fine to coarse. If in doubt, pick a general purpose medium pitch blade. Coarse blades are useful for cutting large cross sections and for dealing with softer materials such as aluminium and plastics. The fine pitch blades are very necessary when dealing with thin section materials such as sheet metals and tubing.

When choosing a blade for a job, try to ensure that at least three teeth are always in contact with the work. This avoids the risk of stripping teeth and gives a smooth cutting action.

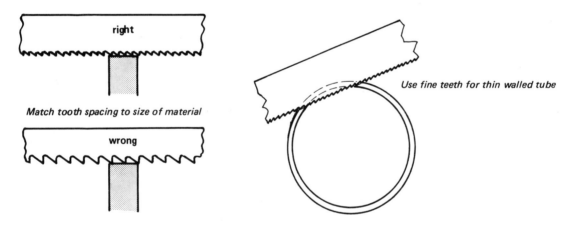

Match tooth spacing to size of material

Use fine teeth for thin walled tube

General sawing technique

Make sure that the work to be cut is securely clamped; the least bit of flexibility will drastically reduce the efficiency of your cutting, and may lead to a broken blade. When sawing very thin metal, it can help to clamp it between two wooden blocks and cut through the wood as well.

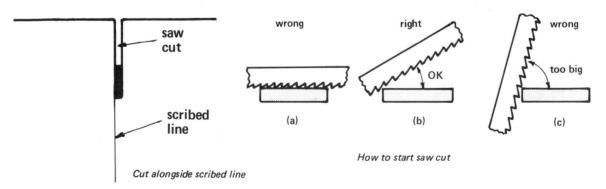

Cut alongside scribed line

How to start saw cut

When marking out the cutting line, do not forget to allow for the width of the blade. Cut alongside the line and not down it; it is easier to keep control of the cut. If the edge of the work is notched with a file it will be found easier to start the saw cut.

Do not start the cut across the entire flat surface of the piece or the blade will slide all over the place; start at an angle to the surface. Too steep an angle will reduce the number of cutting teeth.

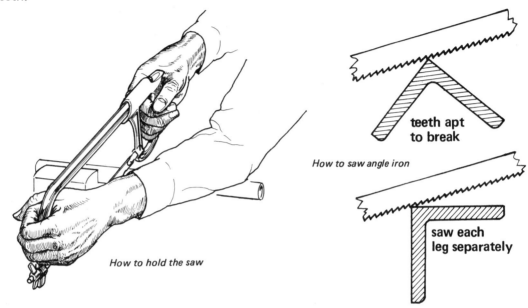

How to hold the saw

teeth apt to break

How to saw angle iron

saw each leg separately

Hold the saw with one hand at each end and apply sufficient pressure on the forward, cutting stroke to keep the teeth working steadily. Too little pressure and the teeth will just wear without doing useful work. Too much pressure and the teeth tend to clog and jam and the cutting efficiency drops sharply. The best pressure can easily be found from the first few cuts; it is fairly obvious when the blade is cutting well.

Use a long steady stroke whenever possible, using all the blade. One complete forward and return stroke per second is a good cutting rate. Anything faster and you'll tire yourself and probably overheat the blade. Short, fast strokes make it much more difficult to follow the cutting line.

Give consideration to supporting the waste piece being cut off. If not, its weight may close the cut, jamming the blade, or tear it open leaving a ragged edge.

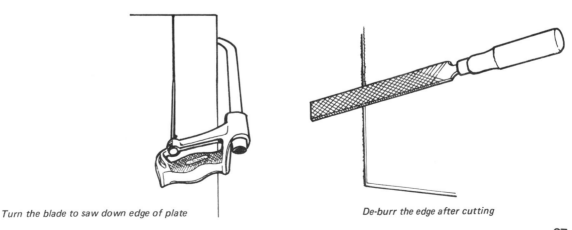

Turn the blade to saw down edge of plate

De-burr the edge after cutting

If you have to make a long cut near the edge of flat material, turn the blade through 90 degrees so that the frame rides outside the piece being cut off.

When you have finished your saw cut, run a file along the edges to remove any burrs.

Other saws

There are a number of other saws which you may find convenient to use besides the basic hacksaw. One valuable ally for the awkward corners is a broken hacksaw blade. To make the manipulation of this a little more convenient, handles can be bought which will guide and clamp a short blade.

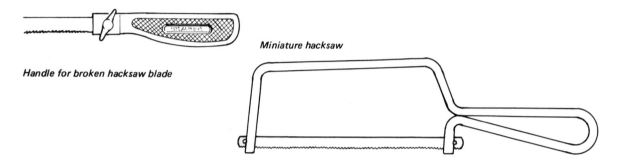

Handle for broken hacksaw blade

Miniature hacksaw

For fine work there is the miniature (junior) hacksaw which relies on the springiness of the frame to hold the small blade in place.

Another useful tool for cutting out awkward shapes in thin materials or in tight corners is the tension file, which is sold under various trade names including Abrafile. As the name implies, this is a cross between a file and a saw. A fine, round spindle cut with file-like teeth is stretched either in a hacksaw or similar frame or between a pair of handles. It is used like a hacksaw but can cut in any direction, allowing the cutting of curves.

Then for the power mad worker, saws can be obtained for attachment to your electric drill. The circular saw is probably too dangerous and rough a tool for general use around your car, but a good jig-saw attachment can be very useful.

Part of a tension file

Be careful with power saws   OOPS!

Like the saw, the file consists of a multiplicity of small cutting tools on a common carrier. It is used for finishing components to size, cutting awkward shapes, and achieving a smooth finish. The basic file consists of a flat blade of steel which has a series of parallel grooves cut in its face. When hardened, the edges of these grooves form the cutting teeth. At one end of the file is a projection, the tang, onto which a wooden handle is fitted. Never use a file without a handle; it is very easy to dig the tang into your hand, with rather gory results.

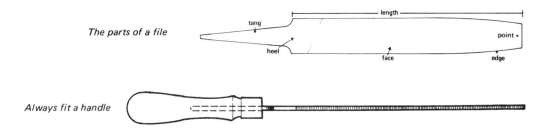

The parts of a file

Always fit a handle

Types of file

The teeth of a file come in two types — single-cut, with one set of parallel teeth, and double-cut where a second set of grooves are cut at an angle to the first. The differences between these are hardly likely to be relevant to your applications. The teeth vary in pitch and depth and are generally known, in order, as rough, bastard, second and smooth cut. Selection is, of course, dependent on the work to be done, heavy cutting on soft material requiring a rougher file than fine work on hard material. The bastard or second cut is usually a good compromise.

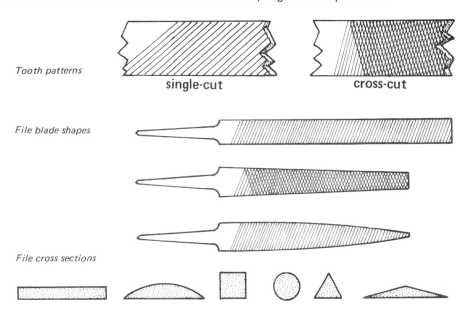

Tooth patterns

single-cut   cross-cut

File blade shapes

File cross sections

The basic flat file comes with parallel, taper and curved sides and, again, for your purposes the choice is probably irrelevant. There are also a number of alternative cross sections which can be useful if you have to work in difficult corners. The round file is necessary if you have to open up a drilled hole, and the triangular file can be useful for finishing off sharp inside corners.

Files come in a variety of sizes, usually being described by their length, cross section and cut (eg 8 inch flat smooth). Very fine files are sometimes referred to as 'rat-tails' or 'swiss files', the latter being an echo of their use in watch making.

Using a file

Firstly, make sure that the work piece is properly secure. Filing is a two-handed job, and if you are working on a loose component you need to clamp it in a vice.

Grip the file handle in one hand and the tip of the file in the other and move it across the work at the same time applying pressure against the face to be cut. Like sawing, a long steady stroke is best, and pressure should be applied on the forward stroke (ie away from you).

Concentrate on keeping the file flat; it is very easy to rock it up and down as you move it backwards and forwards. This results in filing a curved surface instead of a flat one. Of course, if you are trying to cut a curve you will find it very difficult to stop it coming out flat on that occasion!

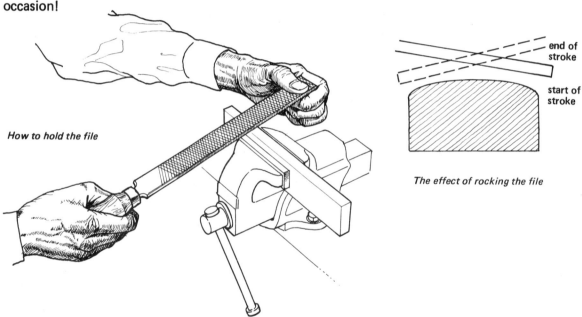

How to hold the file

end of stroke

start of stroke

The effect of rocking the file

Moving the file sideways a little on each stroke avoids cut marks appearing on the work surface. If you are filing the edge of thin material, make the line of your stroke nearly parallel to the edge rather than at right angles. This will give a smoother cutting action.

If it is vital to obtain a good flat surface, you can try your hand at draw-filing. With this technique the file is held across the body, gripped in the two hands. It is placed flat on the surface to be cut and moved away from and towards your body while at the same time pressing it down onto the work. Using this technique it is easier to maintain equal pressure on the two ends and avoid rocking the file.

Most flat files will be found to have teeth cut on one edge only, the other being left smooth. When working into inside corners, make sure that this 'safe' edge is towards the adjacent material so that you do not undercut it unintentionally.

Cleaning the teeth of files is a necessary regular job. It is best done either with a stiff wire brush or a 'file-card', the latter being a mat of wire bristles designed specifically for this job.

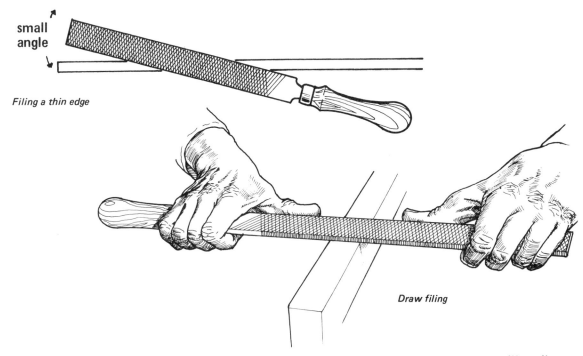

small angle

Filing a thin edge

Draw filing

Files are usually the hardest materials in your tool box. They are brittle and will easily shatter if dropped, and will also mark any other tools against which they rub. So keep them separately packed.

This hardness can sometimes be exploited by unorthodox use of a file. The square end, or the safe edge, of a flat file makes quite a good scraper for cleaning surfaces, and the tapered tang (exposed by pulling off the handle) can be used as a crude taper-reamer for opening up a hole slightly.

General purpose cutting tool

General purpose cutting tool

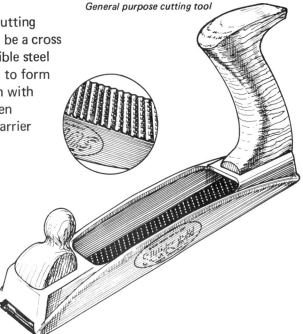

In recent years a type of general purpose cutting tool has been developed which can be said to be a cross between a file and a plane. In this tool a flexible steel blade has been pierced, hardened and ground to form a multiplicity of separate cutting blades, each with its own chip clearance space. This blade is then mounted under tension on various types of carrier to allow its use for either file movements or smoothing plane movements.

This type of tool, often referred to by the trade name of the early brands, 'Surform', is particularly useful on plastics and the softer metals where adequate chipclearance is a problem with coarse files. They can also be useful for edge cutting on plates and other places where the bulk of the tool is not an embarrassment.

Chapter 14 Other Cutters

Cutting tools with progressively more and finer teeth have been dealt with already. In this Chapter we will discuss the logical conclusion to this progression — grinding wheels and abrasive paper. However, before moving on to these, there is one other type of cutting tool which you will find useful and which is included here for lack of anywhere else to put it.

Chisels

The metal cutting chisel, usually called a 'cold chisel', is a piece of steel forged to a blunt point at one end. The pointed end is hardened and ground to a sharp edge which is usually between a half and one inch wide. In use, the chisel is applied to the metal to be cut and struck with a metal faced hammer.

You are likely to find the cold chisel useful for chipping away roughness, protruding welds, or faulty parts, for cutting openings in sheet metal (see Chapter 10) and for cutting away seized-up nuts or bolts.

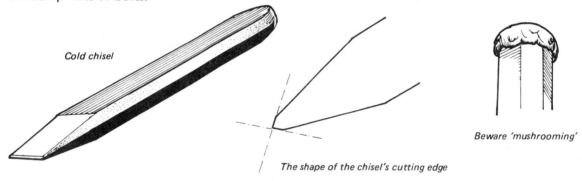

Cold chisel

The shape of the chisel's cutting edge

Beware 'mushrooming'

To give the cutting face adequate strength, it is ground at a fairly blunt angle. As a result it can quickly lose its sharpness if used a lot. Resharpen, with a file or grindstone, to approximately the same angle. After a lot of use there is a tendency for the end which is hit to gradually swell and start to bend over at the edges — called 'mushrooming'. A chisel in this state is dangerous, as fragments can fly off when struck.

You may also come across the 'cold set', which is a chisel with a very narrow face used for cutting grooves, and the 'bolster' with a blade two or three inches wide. Neither of these are likely to be needed in your automobile maintenance. Where there is a need to cut delicate metal-work a cheap carpenter's wood chisel can be a more useful tool than the cruder cold chisel.

Grinding wheels

The grinding processes take advantage of the very hard and sharp corners on some crystalline materials, such as silica (sand), glass, carborundum and emery, and use these as multiple cutting tools. The different processes apply these powders in differing ways. For grinding wheels the 'grit' is bonded together with some form of resin into a wheel form which is mounted on an axle so that it can be rotated. The work to be cut is brought into contact with the rotating grinding wheel and the rapidly moving grit particles gradually cut away the metal. The resin bond is itself designed to wear away and release the particles of grit which become blunted, so that fresh, sharp grit is always being used.

Grits come in a variety of coarsenesses used according to the type of material being cut and the finish required. The rules for selection tend to be the same as for the other cutting tools. Soft materials and heavy cuts require coarse grits at lower speeds; hard materials, smaller cuts and smooth finish require the fine grits at higher speeds.

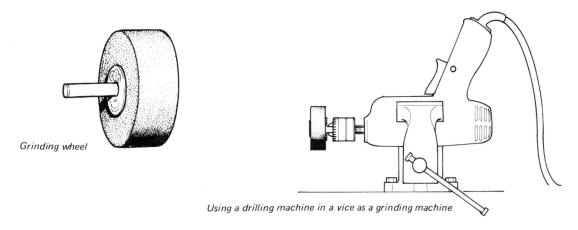

Grinding wheel

Using a drilling machine in a vice as a grinding machine

Bench mounted power or hand driven grinding wheels can be obtained, but for the do-it-yourselfer it is probably better to get a set of wheels which fit the hand electric drill. If it is desired to bring the work to the wheel, the drill can be mounted in a bench stand or clamped in a vice. The same tools can, however, also be used to bring the grinding wheel to the work.

Different shape small grinding wheels

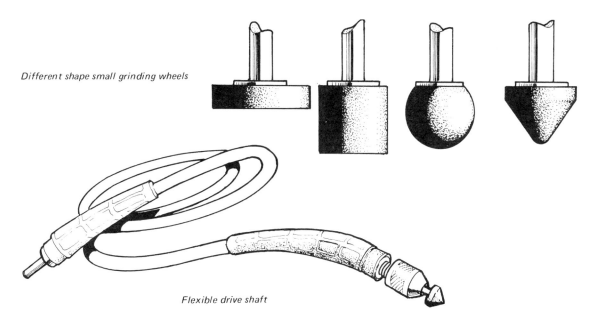

Flexible drive shaft

Grinding wheels come in a variety of shapes, which can be useful for working into awkward corners. Flexible drive shafts can also be obtained, which allow the use of small grinding wheels in very congested locations. Flexible steel discs can be obtained which have a cutting grit bonded to the face. These can be useful for smoothing large flat areas.

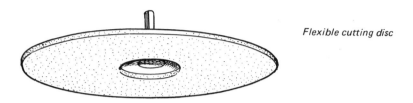

Flexible cutting disc

When using a grinding wheel always wear goggles. Bits of grit, fragments of metal and sparks fly off in all directions. Do not try to take too heavy a cut, and be careful not to overheat the workpiece. You may spoil its mechanical properties.

Abrasive paper and cloth

With these, the abrasive grit is bonded to a flexible backing sheet. Sand and glass are usually bonded to paper, while emery and carborundum are bonded to cloth. The latter are more suitable for use with metals. As for the other abrasives, they come in various grades, sometimes referred to by name — coarse, fine, extra fine — and sometimes by a number. The lower the number, the finer the grit. For example, 00 is smoother than 0.

In use, a convenient size piece is torn off and folded either about itself or about a block of wood. Held in the hand it is then rubbed on the workpiece. In general, one would not attempt to use one of the abrasive cloths for major cutting work. They are usually used after other cutting operations, such as filing or grinding, to obtain a final smooth surface. They will also be used to roughen a polished surface where it is required to get a coat of paint to bond firmly to the surface.

Where it is required to obtain a very smooth final surface, use is made of successively finer grits. For the finest grades you should choose 'wet and dry' emery. The backing of this abrasive maintains its strength even when water soaked, and for final smoothing it is repeatedly dipped in water while being used. The result of this is that the actual cutting is carried out by a water carried paste of abrasive which is pushed over the surface by the cloth. This process can lead to a mirror finish being obtained on components.

Whenever any other cutting operation has been carried out — sawing, drilling, filing — the final de-burring operation should be given by a rub of emery cloth against the cut edges and corners.

Abrasive paste

Carborundum grit mixed with a light grease is used whenever two metal surfaces have to be matched accurately together. The most likely place where you will meet this problem is in re-grinding the seating of the exhaust and inlet valves in your engine. Here, a metal to metal seal must be obtained, and it is achieved by rotating a valve against its seating with an abrasive paste interposed. Handy tins can be obtained with both coarse and fine grade pastes in separate compartments.

Many chapters have made reference to securely holding components, so it is appropriate now to consider the tools involved in this holding — pliers, pipe wrenches, vices and clamps.

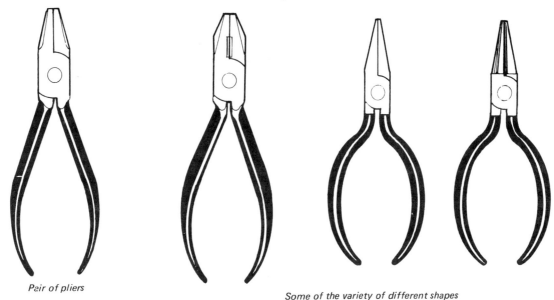

Pair of pliers

Some of the variety of different shapes

Pliers

These consist of two forged steel arms hinged together. Each arm has a short gripping jaw at one end and a long handle at the other. Applying hand pressure to squeeze together the handles grips anything placed between the jaws.

Pliers are made in a great variety of shapes and sizes, with plain jaws, long-nosed, round-nosed, with and without cutting edges and sometimes with rubber or plastic protection on the handles. For your general purpose needs, a very large pair, a medium size pair and a small pair, the latter perhaps with long-nose jaws, would be completely adequate.

Parallel serrated jaws

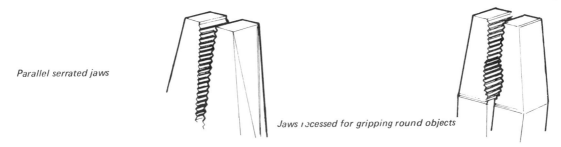

Jaws recessed for gripping round objects

The jaw faces are usually serrated to give maximum gripping effect, and if you are holding something which can be easily marked, the serrations should be padded with plastic, cloth or paper. Some pliers, as well as having the parallel face jaws, have a serrated circular, triangular or oval opening to make the gripping of round objects easier. This is a useful facility and at least one of your pairs of pliers should have this.

Like all hardened and heat treated tools, never heat a pair of pliers as it can completely destroy their strength. Never use them as a hammer and do not overstrain by applying more than the force of one hand. Long nosed pliers are particularly liable to distortion. Keep the hinge well lubricated.

Cutting

Pliers are often provided with cutting edges. These come in two types, both of which can be available on the same pair of pliers. At the side of the hinge, cutting edges can be formed which, moved past each other, give a shearing action. These can be particularly useful for cutting wire.

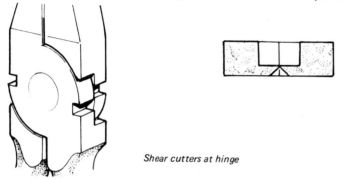

Shear cutters at hinge

The other form is a pair of edges which just meet when the jaws close. The setting of these relative to the gripping faces is a compromise. On some pliers the cutting edges are given priority and when they close there is still a small gap between the gripping faces.

If you are likely to need cutters often, particularly if you are doing quite a lot of wiring, it is probably better to avoid this compromise situation and buy a 'side-cutter'. Here the jaws are formed solely as cutters which are usually angled slightly to the line of the handles to allow the cutting edge to be brought very close to a flat workpiece.

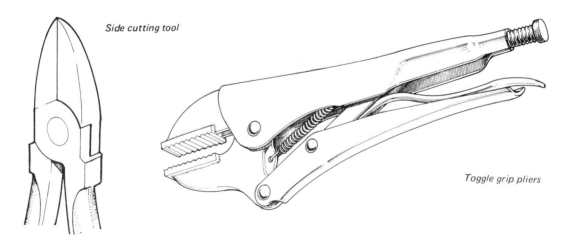

Side cutting tool

Toggle grip pliers

Toggle grip

This specialised development of the pliers is probably best known by the trade name of the original version — the 'Mole Grip'. In this tool the handles are coupled by an adjustable, over-centre latching, or 'toggle' lever. The grip can be used in the normal manner, or by adjusting the setting of the toggle, the final gripping pressure can be arranged to cause the mechanism to latch.

In this position the pressure is maintained on the jaws even when the hand pressure is released, being relaxed only by a trip lever which unlatches the mechanism.

This tool is an invaluable aid. It can be used as a pair of pliers, an adjustable spanner or a portable vice. As the advertisement says — it's like having another hand.

Pipe wrenches

There are a number of tools designed specifically for gripping round objects. Most of them have been developed originally to meet the needs of pipe-fitters, but they are applicable to any situation where it is necessary to apply a rotational force to a round or irregular object.

The simple pipe grip has heavily serrated curved jaws. When squeezed on a pipe and a rotational force applied, there is a wedging action of the curved jaws which tends to increase the gripping force. This action applies only over a limited range of jaw angles, so an adjustable hinge point is provided to cover a wider variation of pipe sizes.

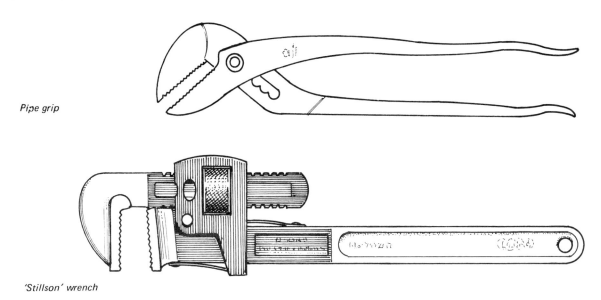

Pipe grip

'Stillson' wrench

The logical development of this wedging action is shown in the patented 'Stillson' wrench. Sometimes mistaken for an adjustable spanner because of its worm adjustment, the moving jaw of the Stillson is designed to rock against the pressure of a spring. An object is gripped by closing up the movable jaw as for an adjustable spanner, but as soon as pressure is applied, the loose jaw rocks and its wedging action is extremely powerful. If you feel like saving up for it, a medium size Stillson is a good friend to have in your tool kit. Very often the Stillson will work when more sophisticated tools have failed.

Pipe-fitters often use, on large diameter pipes, a 'chain wrench'. Using the wedging action again, the movable jaw is replaced by a length of chain which is wrapped around the pipe and then hooked onto the handle. It is unlikely that you would ever need to buy one of these, but the application of the principle could be useful if ever you are faced with, say, an oil filter cover which will just not unscrew. Tie a piece of stout rope to a steel or wooden bar, or other suitable lever. Rest the lever against the component to be gripped and wrap the rope several times around the component. Hold the end of the rope tightly and apply pressure to the lever. This action tightens the rope and can give quite a considerable turning force.

If the object to be turned is very smooth or greasy, it may be found difficult to get a good grip with any of the tools. A useful trick to try here is to wrap a piece of emery cloth or sand paper around the component with the rough side in, and then apply the tool over this.

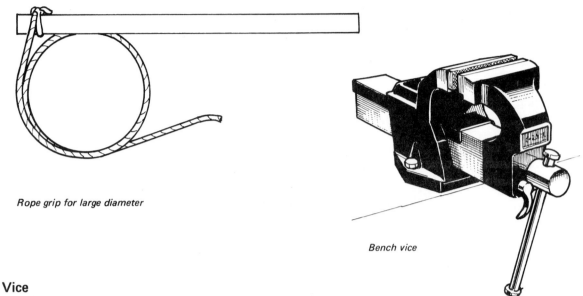

Rope grip for large diameter

Bench vice

Vice

Whatever personal vices you may have, you will also need an engineer's bench vice! This consists of a heavy steel frame, which can be bolted to a bench, and provided with a broad gripping jaw at the top. Into this frame slides another component with a matching jaw. The two are coupled together by a screw provided with a handle at the front. You will need a vice with at least 4 inch wide jaws, and 6 inch would be even better.

Make sure that the vice is securely mounted at the front edge of a solid work bench. If the vice can wobble or move, you will find it very difficult to carry out, with accuracy, many jobs.

To save time winding the screw when you wish to substantially change the jaw position, some vices have a release lever which disengages the nut from the screw allowing the moving jaw to slide freely. The handle is then used only for applying the final pressure.

The basic vice jaw has a hardened insert with a serrated face giving a flat parallel grip.

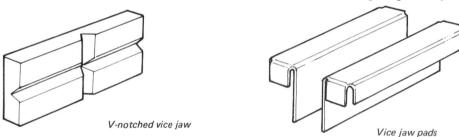

V-notched vice jaw

Vice jaw pads

Alternative jaws are sometimes available which have a V-shape cut-out. These are very useful for gripping round or uneven components. In many cases you cannot risk having a component marked by the vice jaws and they must be padded. The traditional workshop practice is to make up a pair of aluminium or copper pieces which clip over the jaws. It is also possible to buy ready made jaw pads in metal, fibre or plastic.

A good vice is a sturdy object, designed to be used as an anvil sometimes, but nevertheless it should be looked after like any other tool. Keep the slide and screw well lubricated; do not hammer the handle to tighten it up; do not let it get overheated if you are using a blow-lamp nearby.

The carpenter's wooden vice is generally unsuitable for the type of work you will be doing. You will damage the vice by trying to grip metal objects and you will not get the grip which you need.

Wedge-lock

A useful supplementary device on the work-bench is a wedge lock bench clamp. In this device a frame, which has tapering sides, is screwed down onto the bench. On one side of the frame slides a loose jaw which is always parallel to the other side of the frame. As this jaw moves towards the narrow end of the frame the gap between it and the side closes up. A component placed against the sliding jaw and pushed sharply towards the narrow end is gripped securely enough for many minor operations.

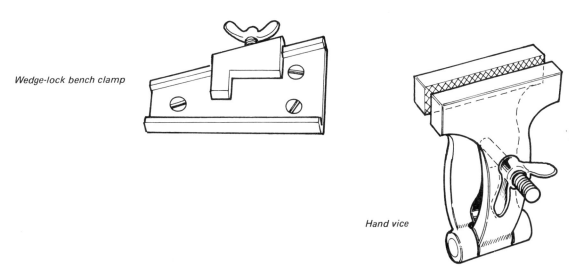

Wedge-lock bench clamp

Hand vice

Hand vice

A hand vice can be a useful tool for gripping small components, although many of its functions can be fulfilled by a toggle-grip pliers. The simple hand vice has small jaws on the end of a pair of legs hinged together. A spring pushes the legs apart against a screw which applies the gripping pressure.

Clamps

Finally, one or two G-clamps are always likely to be useful. The G-clamp consists of a frame in the shape of three sides of a rectangle with a hand-operated screw at one end which can apply pressure to an object held against the other end of the clamp. More complex clamps have adjustable frames which allow them to be used for a wider range of jobs.

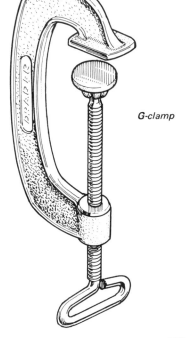

G-clamp

You may feel by this time that you would like to get onto something more energetic, to work off some of your frustrations. So let us now consider how to go about hitting things. First you need something a little heavier and more wear-resistant than your hands for doing the hitting, and there are several tools to choose from.

Engineer's ball pein hammer

Engineer's hammer

The basic hammer consists of a forged steel head mounted on a wooden handle. There are several different designs of hammer head, each developed to meet the needs of a particular trade. The one most suitable for your engineering type of activities is the 'ball-pein' head. This has a main hitting face on one side, usually circular and slightly crowned. Opposite to this is a hemi-spherical face, the ball-pein. A good general purpose hammer would have a one-pound head. A lighter one may occasionally be useful, but if you are going to start hitting your automobile, you will probably need to hit fairly hard. If you are feeling really extravagant you can get hammers forged from alloy steel with an integral steel shaft fitted with a rubber grip; of interest to the professional but probably not worthwhile for you.

Club hammer

Sledge-hammer/club-hammer

Nicknamed 'flogging hammers', these are the tools for real pounding. They come in weights from the two-pound club-hammer to the twenty-pound sledge, and shaft lengths from 12 inches to 36 inches. While you will rarely need to swing a sledge, a small one can be useful as a portable anvil. The inertia of the heavy head is useful for backing up a workpiece which is being hit with the lighter hammer. Used with the head held in the hand it can apply a force in a restricted space where there would not be room to swing another lighter hammer.

Rubber mallet

Rubber mallet

A large head of hard moulded rubber is secured to a wooden handle. This type of tool has the great advantage of not marking the workpiece and is very suitable where an overall force is required rather than a localised pressure. For example, fitting together components which are designed with a close fit.

Copper/leather mallet

Copper/hide mallet

This tool provides a compromise between the steel faced hammer and the rubber mallet. A metal head has a round insert in each end. Usually one is copper and the other a tightly wound spiral of leather (hide). The appropriate face is used according to how harsh you wish to be. Some modern versions of this tool have replaceable plastic inserts instead of the traditional copper/leather, but they are not as effective.

Using a hammer

Make sure that the workpiece is adequately supported. If it is not, the force of the hammer blow will be absorbed by spring action with little effect other than to bounce the hammer back. In the absence of other supports, a sledge hammer held up behind the work can provide a good back-up.

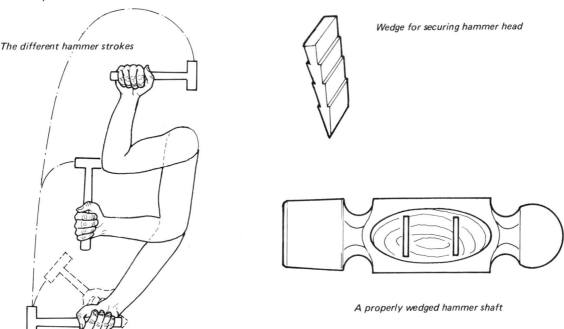

The different hammer strokes

Wedge for securing hammer head

A properly wedged hammer shaft

Adapt your swing to the type of hitting being done. If you require relatively light, accurate taps, swing the hammer by wrist action only. For a stronger, more definite blow, swing from the elbow; and if you are really belting something, use wrist, elbow and shoulder together.

Take care of your hammer. Watch out for cracks in the face; if one should appear, get a new hammer. Make sure that the handle is a tight fit and not cracked. If you have to change a wooden handle, drill out the old one, retaining the wedges. Trim the end of the new handle to match the hole in the steel head, noting carefully the taper on the inside of the hole. When the handle fits in snugly, cut off the surplus and drive in the two wedges to expand the wood.

Panel beating

This is the art of forming a metal panel to complicated curvatures by a process of hammering. To achieve good results requires a lot of practice, but you may be faced with a need to straighten out some bit of bent tin to an acceptable condition.

Do not try to do it too quickly. A lot of small blows is the best way. The shape should be formed between a fairly flat and smooth backing-up tool (your sledge-hammer again?), and the ball-pein of your hammer. A professional panel beater has a whole range of hammers, many of which are needed to get into difficult corners. Without these you will, of course, find yourself restricted in what you can attempt.

The metal may have been stretched and squeezing it back to its original size can be quite tricky and slow, and you may get little ripples which are very difficult to remove. Also watch out for work-hardening with its symptoms of fine cracks beginning to appear (see Chapter 3).

To round out the descriptions of various tools we now come to an assortment of useful items which do not fit under any other heading.

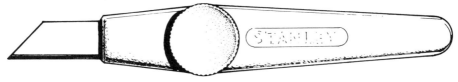

General purpose knife

Knife

You will need a good sharp knife for cutting plastic and rubber, and for scraping surfaces clean. There are a variety of workshop knives available, mostly with replaceable blades.

Dentist's mirror

Mirror

You will need a small mirror for examining awkward corners. A woman's vanity mirror of the size often found in handbags is just about right. A useful refinement is a dentist's mirror on an adjustable handle.

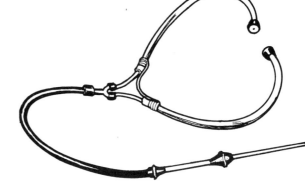

Stethoscope

Stethoscope

Just as a doctor can learn a lot about your state of health by listening to the noises in your chest, so can you develop an ear for the health of your car. The rattle of valve tappets that need resetting; the buzz of a leaking exhaust pipe gasket; the ominous thud of worn main bearings; all of these sounds and many others tell a story. Particularly if you are trying to keep an old car in good health, the investment in a stethoscope is worthwhile. It helps you to separate the rattles that really matter from the general creaks and bangs of old age. While generally similar to a doctor's stethoscope, you can get ones specially designed for engineering use. Often they will have an extension probe for getting into awkward corners.

Inspection lamps

There will be many occasions when you will need extra illumination on your work, particularly if you have to get under the vehicle. Do not use a mains electric lamp on the end of a flex. Apart from the fact that you may need its help when you are away from the garage, the risks of shock and fire if you should break the bulb are too great. The obvious simple alternative is a battery torch or hand lantern. If you are getting a lantern, it is worth getting one which has an alternative red beacon on the top (flashing for preference). If you are broken down at night, a good warning beacon may save a nasty crash. You may feel it is worth fixing up a 12 volt bulb with leads with clips on the end. This can be connected to the battery to give you light on your work, and can also be used as a test lamp (see next Chapter). There are a number of commercially available inspection lamps with protected bulbs which are variants on this theme. These are the best bet.

Battery lantern with warning beacon

Timing lamp

Also known as a 'strobe light', this usually consists of a neon lamp with a pair of leads fitted with clips. With one lead connected to the vehicle earth and the other connected to one of the ignition leads, the lamp will flash every time that the ignition lead is energised. Because this flashing is exactly synchronised to the movement of the engine, any moving component which is illuminated only by the lamp will appear to be stationary. Most vehicle manuals give details of how to use a timing lamp for checking ignition timing settings.

Flange puller

For many jobs which involve getting inside the machinery, and for some models, just to replace brake linings, you will find yourself faced with a flange, coupling, pulley or gear wheel which is a tight push fit on a shaft and which must be removed. You may be able to hit it from behind with a mallet, or even get a lever between it and an adjacent bit of ironmongery to apply the necessary pressure, but failing these, you will need a flange puller. This usually consists of a central boss with three or more hinged arms. Each of these arms is hooked at the end. In the centre of the boss is a long screw. To use the puller, it is placed in front of the flange and the arms hooked behind the flange. Tightening up the screw now applies pressure to the shaft in the centre and the puller, together with the flange, is forced off.

In an emergency you can sometimes make a puller to fit the particular job. For example, if the flange has bolt holes, these can be used to loosely attach a plate which has the pressure screw in the centre. If you have not got suitable tools for tapping the central hole, the effect can be

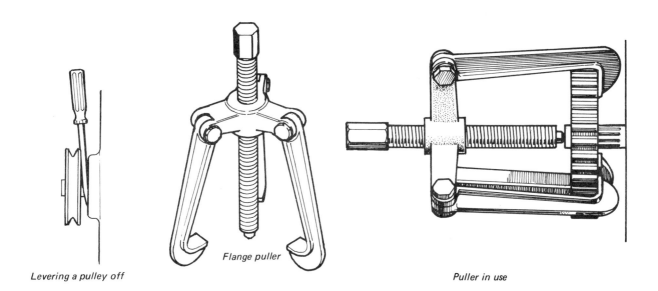

Levering a pulley off

Flange puller

Puller in use

achieved by using a nut on the screw in front of the plate. In the absence of suitable bolt holes in the flange, it is usually possible to place a pair of loose straps behind, attached to the plate in front (see diagram).

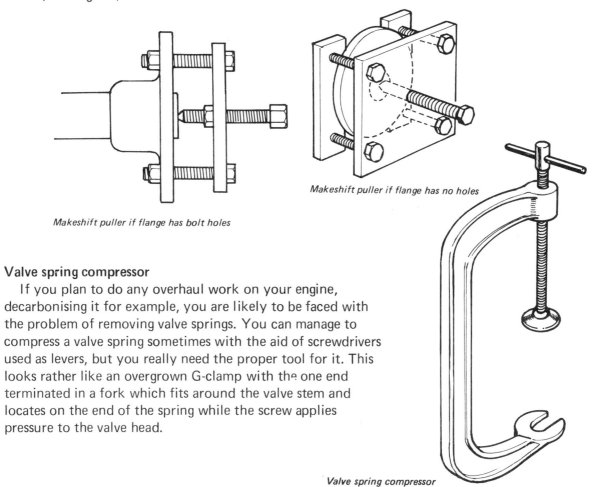

Makeshift puller if flange has bolt holes

Makeshift puller if flange has no holes

Valve spring compressor

If you plan to do any overhaul work on your engine, decarbonising it for example, you are likely to be faced with the problem of removing valve springs. You can manage to compress a valve spring sometimes with the aid of screwdrivers used as levers, but you really need the proper tool for it. This looks rather like an overgrown G-clamp with the one end terminated in a fork which fits around the valve stem and locates on the end of the spring while the screw applies pressure to the valve head.

Valve spring compressor

Piston ring clamp

If your overhauling goes even further and you get the pistons out, you will need a piston ring clamp to get them back. This is a band of steel with a screw tightening device. Placed around the piston rings and the screw tightened up, the clamp squeezes the rings in far enough for them to be pushed back into the cylinder. If you have four hands and ample patience you can probably manage without this item.

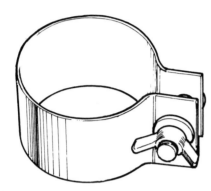

Piston ring clamp

There is no intention here of trying to teach you how to be an electrical engineer. If you want to know the details of auto-electrics, which is a complex and specialised study, you are going to need other books than this. All that is being included here are a few basics and some hints to help you with the simple jobs.

Basic theory

An electric current flows when electrons move between atoms. Now, while that statement is true, it is not going to be of much use to you. It is perhaps easiest to take a simple analogy with a water pipe system.

To make water flow through pipes you need to apply pressure. This can be done by using a pump or having a storage tank above the pipe, or by a combination of both. It is more difficult (needs more pressure) to get the same amount of water through a small pipe. The water flows easier through a smooth pipe.

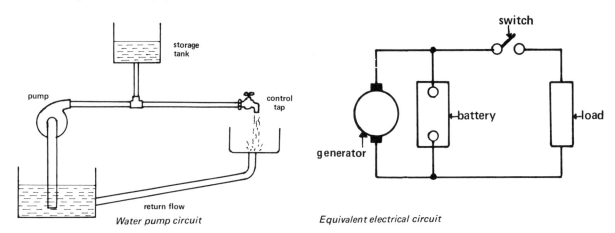

Water pump circuit   Equivalent electrical circuit

In an electrical circuit the current flow is measured in 'amps' (named after an early electrical scientist Ampere). The pressure required to cause that current to flow is measured in 'volts' (named after another scientist, Volta). The source of the pressure (volts) to cause the current (amps) to flow is a generator (the equivalent of the pump) or a storage battery (the equivalent of the tank). The friction (or resistance) which opposes the flow of the current is measured in ohms (yes, another man called Ohm). To reduce the resistance we use 'high conductivity' materials, which are always metals, the best being copper.

In the same way that rubbing friction causes heat, so the resistance to an electric current causes heat. If we take a very thin piece of high resistance metal and connect it in an electrical circuit it will get very hot; so hot that it may start to glow or even become white hot. This is the basis for the electric lamp. The electric motor is the reverse of a generator and you need not concern yourself with the theory other than to note that if a wire with a current flowing in it is placed near a magnet, there will be a force trying to move the wire. Conversely, if you move a wire near a magnet, an electric current is generated in the wire.

An electric circuit must always be completed back to the source. Usually a battery or generator will have its terminals marked positive (+) and negative (−) and the current is always considered to flow from the positive terminal through the circuit and back to the negative. At any time the current can be stopped from flowing by breaking this closed circuit. It is possible to have several devices 'in series' in a circuit; this is quite usual for controlling switches, the operation of any one breaking the ciruit. It is also possible to have devices connected in parallel;

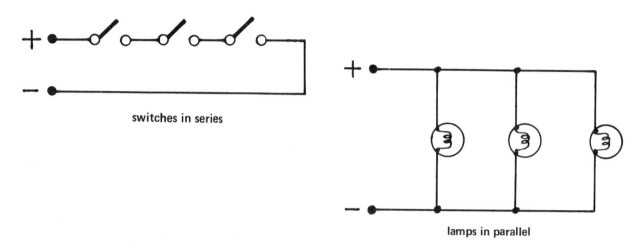

switches in series

lamps in parallel

this is the usual arrangement for lamps and other loads. You will also find series/parallel combinations used. The implications of these methods of connection will become apparent later. In the automobile it is normal practice for the circuit to be completed through the metal of the vehicle shell, usually referred to as the 'earth' connection. On older vehicles the positive side of the battery and generator was tied to earth, but modern vehicles have the negative earthed. It is important to watch out for this change.

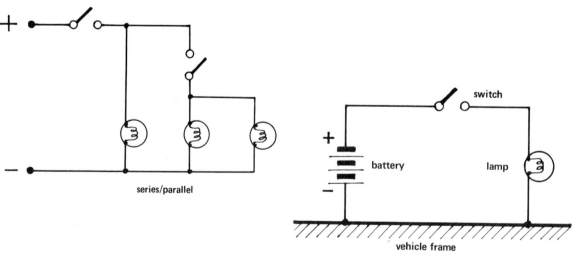

series/parallel

vehicle frame

Use of vehicle frame to complete the circuit

There are two simple formulae which you will need to remember. The first is known as Ohm's law, and states that voltage is equal to current multiplied by resistance (using standard symbols, $V = IR$). You will not often have to put figures to this formula, but rather just consider its implications. For example, one lamp with resistance R, connected to a supply of

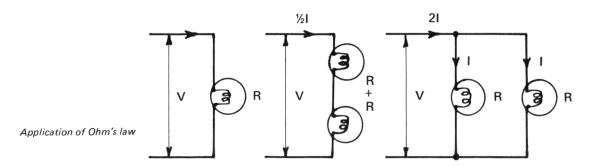

Application of Ohm's law

voltage V, will draw a current of I amps. Connect two lamps in series (2R) and the current is reduced to ½I. Connect two lamps in parallel and the current increases to 2I.

The second formula states that the power used in a device, measured in watts (you guessed it, James Watt), is given by the voltage multiplied by the current. In automobile practice, with a few very old exceptions, the voltage is always 12. So, if we connect a 60 watt fog lamp bulb into a 12v circuit, we will get a 5 amp current flowing (60 = 12 x 5).

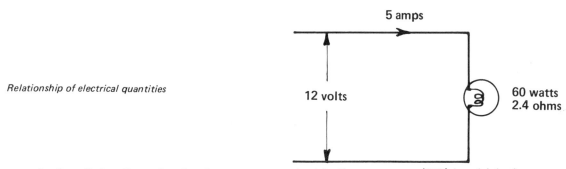

Relationship of electrical quantities

So far all the discussion has been concerned with direct current (DC) in which the current flows in only one direction. There is also alternating current (AC) in which the direction of current flow reverses many times per second. This is the type of electricity system used in your household mains supply, with the reversals taking place 50 times per second. Recently, automobile manufacturers have replaced the DC generator, a dynamo, with an alternator which produces AC. The reasons for this change are technically complex and not relevant for discussion here. However, you need not let this change worry you, because built into the frame of the alternator is a 'rectifier' which converts the AC to DC. The external circuitry, which is all you will be interested in, is therefore still basically the same.

*Internal connections of
DC generator and AC alternator*

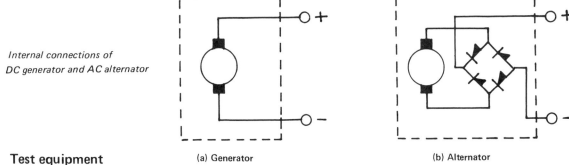

(a) Generator   (b) Alternator

Test equipment

It is desirable that you have some means of checking circuits for continuity and the presence of a supply voltage. The simplest test equipment for this is a lamp and some lengths of wire. Obtain a 12 volt lamp with holder. Suitable ones are sold as interior illumination lamps or inspection lamps, or you may be able to obtain a lamp holder without any extra trimmings.

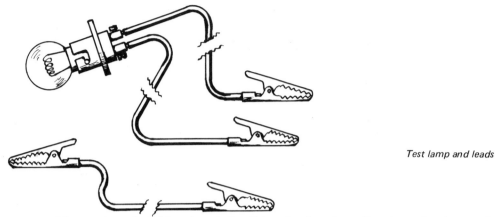

Test lamp and leads

Connect to this two lengths of insulated, flexible wire (see later for size selection and connecting instructions), each about 3 feet long. On the ends of the leads fit spring-loaded 'crocodile clips'. Cut another length of wire about 3 feet long and fit a crocodile clip at each end. You now have your test kit.

If you wish to test circuits to see if they are 'live', clip one of the lamp leads onto the vehicle frame ('earth') and use the other as a probe. If a wire is live, the lamp will light when

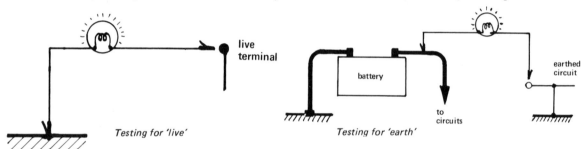

Testing for 'live' *Testing for 'earth'*

contact is made. To test for earthed circuits, clip one lamp lead to the battery or other live terminal. The lamp will light whenever the other lamp lead is touched on an earthed circuit.

To test a circuit for continuity, first check if it is live. If it is live at one end and not at the other, there is no continuity through the circuit. If the circuit is not live, check if it is earthed.

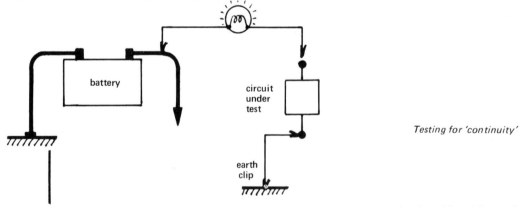

Testing for 'continuity'

Again, if it is earthed at one end and not at the other, there is no continuity. If neither of these tests lights the lamp, take the loose lead and clip one end to earth and the other to one end of the circuit to be tested. If this earth does not now appear at the other end of the circuit under test there is no continuity.

If you plan to carry out other electrical work around the house, perhaps radio or electronics work, you may think it is worth investing in an electrical testmeter. Get one of the multi-purpose instruments where one meter can be used for many different measurements by manipulating switches on the instrument. It should be suitable at least for DC measurements up to 15 volts and 20 amps, and for resistance (or continuity) measurements.

The automobile electrical system

The prime source of electricity on an automobile is a generator (dynamo or alternator) driven from the engine. Obviously this can supply power only when the engine is running, so to provide for needs when the engine is stopped, a 'battery' is connected into the circuit. This is usually a 'lead/acid accumulator' consisting of six 'cells' connected electrically in series. As each cell is rated at 2 volts, the full voltage of the battery is 12 volts. As current is drawn from the battery (it is 'discharged'), a chemical reaction takes place internally, changing the cell materials. If the generator now pushes current in the reverse direction ('charging' the battery), the chemical reaction is reversed, restoring the cell materials to their original form.

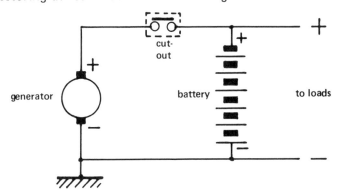

Main power supply circuit

Generator and battery are connected in parallel so that when the engine is running the generator supplies the electrical load and at the same time keeps the battery fully charged. If the engine is now stopped, the battery will automatically continue to supply the load but starts to discharge and gradually to run down. The length of time taken to discharge a battery will depend on the size of the load and the condition of the battery. If you leave your headlights full on, connected to a four year old battery, you need not expect to find much life after a couple of hours. A DC generator which is stopped would provide a very rapid discharge path for the battery, so a special device called the 'cut-out' is interposed between them and disconnects the generator as soon as it has slowed down so far that the battery starts to push current back through it. In the case of the alternator, the built-in rectifiers prevent this current backflow and the cut-out is not required. As soon as the engine is started after a period of battery discharge, the generator will immediately push current into the battery to recharge it, as well as picking up the other loads.

Of course, the engine speed will change quite a lot while you are driving, and without any further control the voltage from the generator would change as well. Another special device, the voltage regulator, is therefore fitted in order to keep the output voltage from the generator fairly steady.

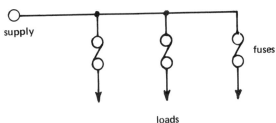

Connection of fused circuits

These then are the power sources and they are connected via a common supply wire to the various loads. Two special loads, the ignition system and the starter are dealt with separately later; all the remaining loads — lamps, heater, wiper motor, radio, instruments — are supplied via fuses. If a component breaks down it may result in a short circuit. This state is equivalent to connecting a live lead straight to earth. There is no significant amount of resistance in the circuit and a very heavy current will flow. This current will cause severe burning at the original failure point and may heat up the supply cables sufficiently to start a fire somewhere else as

Fuse

well. The fuse is a deliberately inserted weak spot in the circuit, so arranged that if the current exceeds a certain value a thin metal strip melts and isolates the faulty circuit. Fuses are removable from their clip mounting and come in various ratings indicated by figures on the fuse body and sometimes by a colour code as well. Always keep a couple of spare fuses adjacent to the fuse box.

Wiring diagram

The way in which your vehicle's electrics are wired up will be recorded by wiring diagrams in the vehicle manual and you must learn to read these. At first sight they look terribly complex, but they are built up from a number of quite separate circuits. You should quite quickly be able to identify the generator/battery group, the ignition system, the starter circuit and then the separate circuits for headlamps, side/tail lamps, horn, flashing indicators, panel lamps, reversing lamps, instrument lamps, etc.

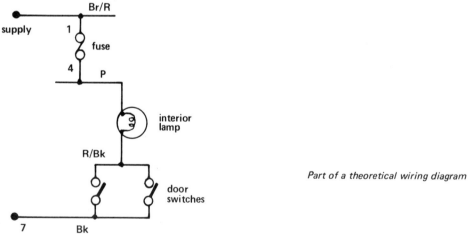

Part of a theoretical wiring diagram

Wiring diagrams are of two types — the theoretical and practical diagrams. In the first case symbols represent the various devices and they are laid out with their wiring to show the circuits clearly and separately without any consideration for the physical locations. In the practical diagram emphasis is placed on the layout of components, the direction of cable runs and the positioning of terminals.

In theoretical diagrams, wires which are joined together are connected anywhere on the diagram which is convenient, the junction being indicated by a black blob at the meeting point of the lines. If two lines cross without a blob, it means there is no connection between them.

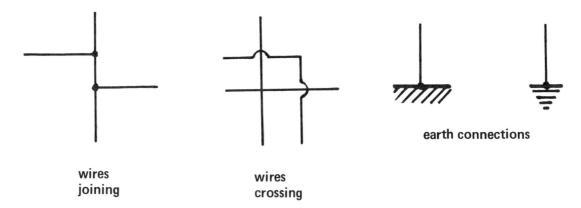

wires joining

wires crossing

earth connections

On some diagrams this is made even clearer by putting a loop in one line to make it look as if it jumps over the other. Sometimes, multiple contacts which are all on the same switch will be scattered around the diagram linked by only a dotted line or even a written reference. The common earth return is often omitted from the diagram as a complete circuit. Any wire which is earthed is just terminated in an earth symbol at the most convenient place on the diagram. The theoretical diagram is easy to follow to identify the different circuits and functions, but as already noted, it has no direct relation to how the vehicle is actually wired. For this we must turn to the practical diagram. Very often the theoretical diagram will carry terminal numbers and wire colour codes which give a direct link to the corresponding information on the practical diagram.

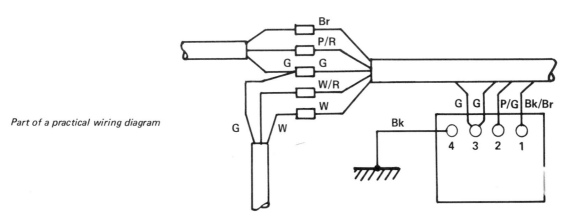

Part of a practical wiring diagram

On the practical diagram the various components are positioned in approximately their correct relationship to each other, and all the terminals are identified so that you can locate them correctly. Wires are indicated separately only where they actually run as a single wire. Much of the vehicle's wiring will be in 'cable harnesses' — bundles of wires together, and these will be indicated as such on the practical wiring diagram. The wires are colour coded to identify their function in the circuits, and these codings are given on the diagram adjacent to the end of each connection.

Some connections, such as earth and main supply leads, go to several terminals. All of these terminals except the last in the line will have two or more wires of the same colour. The angle of the line from the terminal usually gives some indication of which direction the wire will run in a harness. A small rectangular box with two or more lines coming from it usually indicates a plug connection where the wires can be separated. Groups of these will be found where harnesses meet.

Cable rating and colour coding

When making alterations or additions to an automobile's wiring, there is an awful temptation to grab any old bit of wire and just sling it in; after all you want to see how that new fog lamp works! — you can always tidy it up afterwards. But, of course, the tidying up never happens. Much better to get it right first time. Firstly, the cable size must be adequate for the current which is to be carried. The standard automobile cable sizes and their current ratings are given below.

Cable	Current
120/.012	80 amps
84/.012	50 amps
44/.012	27 amps
28/.012	17 amps
14/.010	6 amps

The first figure for the cable denotes the number of individual strands of wire in the cable and the second figure denotes the strand diameter. For example, a 28/.012 cable will be made up of 28 strands of wire, each strand 0.012 inch in diameter.

To determine the current rating you will usually need to use the wattage formula quoted earlier. For example, a 60 watt fog lamp will draw 60 ÷ 12 = 5 amps, and 14/.010 cable would be adequate for connecting this up. However, if you connect two lamps in parallel, then the current is 10 amps and you would need a 28/.012 cable to carry this current properly without heating.

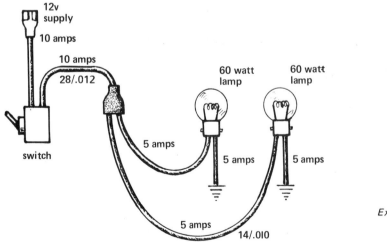

Example of current values

Where there are long runs of cable you will suffer from a voltage drop in the cable itself, and where cables are grouped together they tend to get hotter. So for both of these reasons a larger size of cable should be considered if you are coming anywhere near the limiting rating. For example, a rear window heater which draws 5 amps should be connected with 28/.012 cable for safe working. If in doubt, use a larger size.

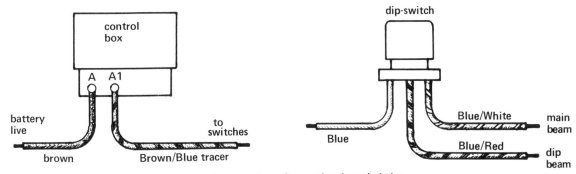

Introduction of tracer colour after passing through device

All the wiring in an automobile is colour coded and you should stick to these colours as far as possible if you make any changes. It can avoid confusion for electricians who may have to do work on your vehicle. The system adopted on British vehicles is fairly straightforward once you get the hang of it. Main supply cables have one colour only. Wires between switches and devices use the main colour plus a tracer colour (a spiral colour line along the cable). Earth cables are black. Units which have the control on the earth side of the circuit (such as the horn, fuel gauge, etc) have a cable colour which is traced with black. The following colours are usually used:

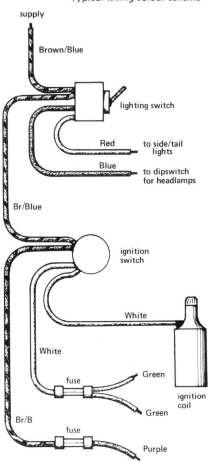

Typical wiring colour scheme

Brown — Main battery and generator circuits. Used for the feed from battery live to the main portion of the wiring harness and voltage regulator unit.

White — Ignition switch controlled circuits not fused. Feeds ignition coil, electric fuel pump, fuse panel supply.

Green — Ignition switch controlled circuits fuse protected. Feeds flashers, stop lamps, gauges, wiper and heater motors, etc.

Purple — Auxiliary fuse protected circuits not controlled by the ignition switch. For interior lights, radio and other items which may be required when ignition is not on.

Blue — Main headlamp feed circuits from lighting switch to dip switch.

Red — Side and tail lamp circuits; panel lights.

Yellow — Overdrive circuits.

Black — All earth circuits.

These basic colours are modified by the tracer colours as indicated in the diagram. If you are connecting in new equipment, choose a colour for the cable which fits the existing pattern and be careful where you connect into existing circuits. You may have correctly chosen the cable size for your new device but overloaded the existing wiring. If in doubt go right back to the fuse box.

So far all the discussion has been of normal standard insulated cables. On some modern automobiles you will find the instrument panel wiring is in the form of a printed circuit. In this the connections are formed by metal film patterns printed onto a flexible plastic strip. These can be fairly easily damaged, and there is no way for you to alter their circuits. They are usually specially identified on the wiring diagram.

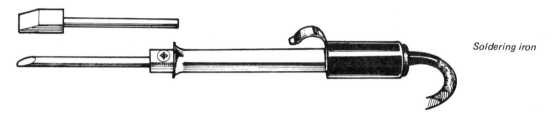

Soldering iron

Soldering

Sooner or later you are likely to need to do some soldering amongst your electrics, either for new connections or for repairs; so a few words here are appropriate. You will need a soldering iron and solder. An electrically heated iron is the best. These consist of an insulated handle, the electrical heating element, and the 'bit', the actual working surface, usually made of copper. For good results it is important that the bit should weigh considerably more than the component being soldered, in order to get fast heat transfer. You should therefore avoid the lightweight irons designed for use on electronic circuits, and get one with a heavy bit and a 60—100 watt heater.

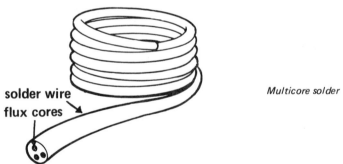

solder wire
flux cores

Multicore solder

Solder is a low-melting-temperature alloy of tin and lead with occasionally other alloying elements. You should get a high tin content resin-cored solder wire. In this, the solder is in the form of wire, a suitable size being 12 SWG, with one or more longitudinal cavities containing a resin flux. When heated, the surfaces of most metals oxidise and it is not possible to get the solder to flow and bond onto the metal. The resin flux when heated attacks the oxide and chemically cleans the metal as the solder is melted onto it. When the soldering iron is heated it is first necessary to 'tin' the bit. This is done by rubbing the end of the solder wire over the working face until the flux has cleaned the surface and left a pool of shining molten solder. If the solder just gathers in a globule it is not properly 'wetting' the surface and if the flux will not clean it, wipe off the excess solder and give the bit a quick rub with a file.

With the bit properly tinned, bring the first of the components to be soldered up to the iron. Let us suppose that it is the end of a stranded cable which is to be soldered into a socket.

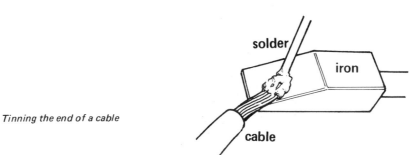

Tinning the end of a cable

Dip the end of the wire into the molten pool of solder on the bit to give a rapid transfer of heat. Touch the heated wire with the end of the solder wire so that new flux is melted out to clean the wire end. The solder should run onto the wire and flow amongst the strands, tinning them all. Shake off any excess molten solder. This tinning operation must be carried out quickly with plastic insulated cables, as the heat spreads rapidly down the copper wires and will start melting the insulation.

Repeat the tinning operation for the socket into which the cable is to fit. When this operation is complete, enter the cable into the socket while at the same time heating both. If the tinning operations have been carried out correctly, the solder on the two surfaces will flow together, perhaps needing a little more to be melted in to fill up the last crevices. Never try to achieve a solder bond in one step; it is too difficult to ensure that all the surfaces are properly scoured by the hot flux.

Cable connections

Whether joining two cables together or connecting a cable to a terminal, there is always the requirement to cut back the insulation from the cable end. Beware the obvious method of making a knife cut around the insulation at the point required. With the fine stranded wire usually used on automobiles, it is very easy to cut through the outer layers of strands as well as the insulation, resulting in the loss of perhaps 20/30% of the cable cross section at the end. With the plastic covered wire which is the usual on modern vehicles, a safe technique is to cut around the insulation but not deeply enough to reach the wire. Then repeatedly bend the cable sharply where the cut has been made. Usually the plastic will crack right through and the sleeve to the end of the wire can then be pulled clear. With some of the older cables with a braided insulation

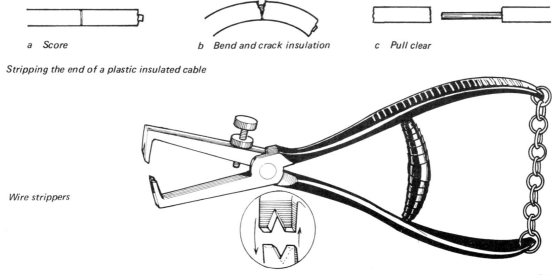

a   *Score*   b   *Bend and crack insulation*   c   *Pull clear*

Stripping the end of a plastic insulated cable

Wire strippers

there is little alternative but care, unless you invest in a proper wire stripping tool. This has notched jaws which can be set accurately to cut to a depth sufficient to cut the insulation but not the wire strands, and while the jaws are still closed the tool is pulled away, stripping the cut insulation off.

The most common methods of terminating cables are listed below.

Screw clamp

For this type the cable insulation is simply stripped back a very short distance and the wire strands are pushed into a hole in the device terminal. A screw is tightened up which comes in sideways into the hole and grips the wire. Often the hole will be made large enough to take two or more cables. If only one is being fitted, strip enough insulation to allow the strands to be folded back on themselves to fill up the space in the terminal. A finger twist of the end of the cable when the insulation has been removed will consolidate the strands and ensure that they all get into the hole.

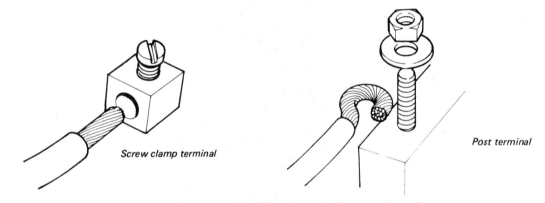

Screw clamp terminal

Post terminal

Post and washers

Again, the cable simply needs to be stripped back a short distance. The strands are then wrapped around the terminal post and a washer placed on top of them followed by a nut to clamp everything tight. Sometimes a screw is used instead of a threaded post with nut. This is not a very satisfactory termination for a multi-stranded cable as it is difficult to adequately grip all the strands. Always wrap the cable clockwise around the post so that tightening the nut tends to pull the loop closer.

Tag terminal

A better way of connecting to a post type of terminal is by using a 'tag' on the end of the cable. This is essentially a washer extended on one side with a grip, into which the end of the cable is soldered. Some types are designed to grip tightly on the cable by squeezing with pliers without the aid of solder, but these are effective only if the insulation is gripped as well. Their fixing then is the same as the push-on type discussed later.

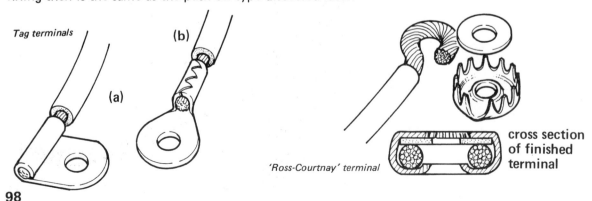

Tag terminals

(b)

(a)

'Ross-Courtnay' terminal

cross section of finished terminal

Ross-Courtenay terminal

A very reliable way of terminating stranded cables without solder for attaching to a post or screw on a component. The 'Ross-Courtenay' consists of two parts — a grooved washer surrounded by a ring of 'claws', and a plain circular washer. The stripped end of the cable is laid around the groove in the lower component, the plain washer is laid on top and the claws are bent over. Applying pressure with a pair of pliers consolidates the whole into a firm termination.

Push-on spade terminal

The most commonly used type of termination on the modern automobile (often known as a Lucar clip). The component has a simple flat blade of metal protruding while the cable terminal has wrap-around spring fingers which grip the flat blade when pushed on. A positive location is given by a small protrusion on the cable terminal which springs into a hole on the flat blade. A plastic or rubber insulating cover is provided which must be pushed onto the cable **before** attaching the terminal. A very small amount of insulation is stripped from the end of the cable; the strands of wire are then pushed under a bridge piece on the terminal and soldered in place.

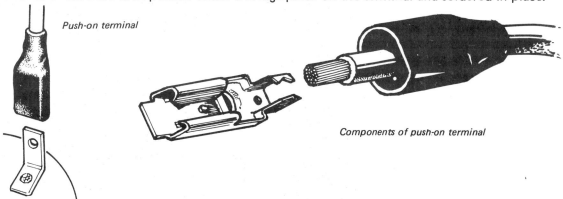

Push-on terminal

Components of push-on terminal

A pair of claws are then squeezed in with pliers to bite into the insulation and relieve the soldered joint of any mechanical strain. Finally, the insulating hood is pulled forward over the terminal. Versions of this terminal are available which will grip the wire strands by squeezing jaws very tightly around the wire. To be reliable they must be squeezed up very tightly and the insulation grip is even more important.

Taper-lock

A variant of the push-on terminal sometimes found, which relies on slightly tapered sides to grip the blade rather than spring pressure on the face. Otherwise they are treated in the same manner.

Bullet terminal

Bullet connector

Usually used for joining the ends of two or more cables together. The end of the cable is stripped back a little way and a 'bullet' is fitted on. The bullet is a hollow piece of tinned copper with a round nose at one end and an indentation just behind. The cable is inserted until the strands just come out through the nose of the bullet. The cable and bullet are then soldered together, the nose being smoothed off with a file afterwards. The tail of the bullet should be overlapping the insulation and is squeezed in with pliers to grip it.

For a straight connection of two cables fitted with bullets, they are pushed into opposite ends of a spring sleeve which has projections to match the indentations in the bullets. The spring

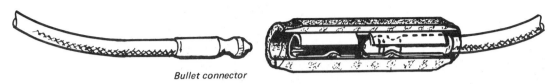
Bullet connector

connector has an outer insulating sleeve which protects the complete junction. Four way connectors can be obtained as well as two way and are often used to provide for the future connection of accessories.

Ignition system

The ignition system is concerned with providing sparks in the engine cylinders at the correct instant to ignite the petrol/air mixture. This is achieved by generating a very high voltage impulse, up to 30,000 volts, which sparks across the gap at the end of the spark plug. The high voltage is produced by the 'ignition coil'. A current from the battery/generator circuit is passed through the 'primary' winding of the coil. At the moment that this 'primary current' is interrupted, a high voltage pulse is emitted from the 'secondary' winding and is directed to the appropriate spark plug by the rotating arm of the 'distributor'. The interruption of the primary current at the correct instant is carried out by the 'contact breaker', a spring loaded switch which is opened by a cam driven from the engine. For the ignition system to function correctly, the primary current must flow properly, the contact breaker must operate at the correct instant, and the high voltage pulse must be directed to the correct cylinder without leakage.

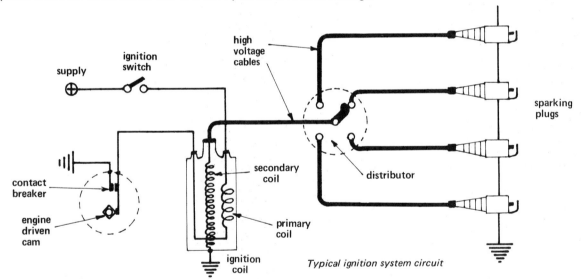
Typical ignition system circuit

The primary circuit must have good contact all the way through, as for any of the other of the vehicle's circuits. Make sure that wire ends and terminals are clean before making connections. The contact breaker contacts (or 'points') must be clean, flat and correctly meeting. There is a lot of wear on these points and they need regular maintenance, so pay particular attention to the instructions given in the vehicle maintenance manual. The setting of the contact breaker gap and the ignition timing will also be covered in your manual and must be kept up to standard. Faulty ignition timing can seriously affect the performance and fuel consumption of the engine.

The high voltage circuit starts at the secondary terminal of the ignition coil and carries through the distributor to the spark plugs. For the whole of this circuit, very strong insulation is required with long surface distances to stop the current leaking away. Keep the external surfaces of the insulators clean and protected from water; also check the interior surface of the distributor cap. The layout of some engine compartments makes the high voltage system rather vulnerable to water spray, which can cause engine failure after hitting a pool of water. Of particular relevance for this type of vehicle, although also useful for others, is a silicone insulation spray which gives wiring and insulators a water repellent coating.

To avoid radio interference, all vehicles are now required to be fitted with 'suppressors'. These are high resistances which are connected in series with the ignition lead. They may be integral in each spark plug cap, in the common lead to the distributor, or in the distributor cap itself. If you cannot see an obvious separate device in this circuit, it is quite likely that resistive leads have been used. These look externally like ordinary ignition cable, but instead of a stranded wire core the central connection is made with a carbon impregnated thread which combines the functions of resistance and connection. This type of cable should not be replaced by wire cable. Not only will you upset the design conditions, but you are liable to find yourself being picked up by the police for radio interference.

Starter system

All modern automobiles are fitted with electric starters. Power is drawn from the battery to drive an electric motor which is geared to the flywheel of the engine. The starter motor requires a very heavy current to operate it; up to 600 amps on a cold morning when the engine is stiff. It therefore has its own large supply cables running by the shortest route direct from the battery.

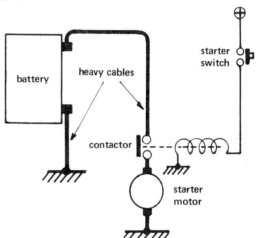

Typical starter motor circuit

Somewhere in this cable run, often at the starter itself, will be a controlling switch (or 'contactor'). Sometimes this will be operated mechanically, but usually it is operated by an electromagnet (or 'solenoid') energised by the starter switch on the instrument panel. Because of the very heavy current in this circuit, it is of vital importance that connection resistance is kept as low as possible. All contact faces must be cleaned very carefully before making joints; terminals must be tightened up securely; and on older cars the main switch contacts should be examined for pitting and burning, and cleaned up if necessary.

The starter motor is disengaged from the flywheel while the engine is running. On older vehicles this is achieved by the 'inertia' or 'Bendix' drive. In this, the inertia of the motor gear wheel as the motor is started is used to throw the gear into engagement; as soon as the engine fires and overruns the starter motor, a spring pushes the gear out of engagement. Many modern vehicles use a 'pre-engagement' starter. In this, the starter gear is moved into engagement with the flywheel gear before the starter is energised. This can be achieved by a direct mechanical control, such as a pull wire, or by an electromagnet. In both cases the last bit of the movement also closes the contacts to energise the starter motor.

Whatever job you tackle on your vehicle, you will be faced with the problems of dirt. At best it will be just caked mud; at worst it can be a horrible oily sludge which seeps into every crack. So a few hints on how to deal with the problem will not go amiss.

Coarse cleaning

Before starting a job, remove the superficial muck from the area where you are going to work; it will make it much pleasanter for you to work, you will be able to see better what you are doing and it minimises the risk of dirt entering any hole you open up.

Road mud can be easily shifted with a strong water jet from a hose pipe, finished off by brushing with a stiff bristle brush. Rusty surfaces should be given a good going over with a wire brush, followed by some repainting when your job is finished. Wear goggles when wire brushing; rust in the eyes is not recommended.

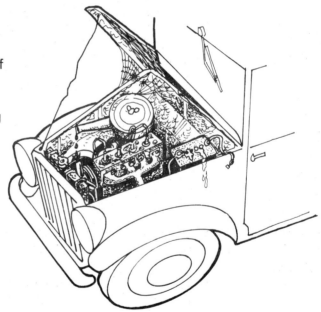

The mess which accumulates around the engine is another problem altogether. The engine compartment always tends to contain an oil mist and this helps dust, insects, bits of paper, etc. to adhere to every surface. Particularly with older engines, this is also aggravated by straight oil leaks. The resulting sticky sludge is difficult to shift.

Get a piece of metal about 2 inches wide, or a proper scraper, and first remove the big lumps of goo from the area you are going to work in. By the way, you had better interpret that 'working area' pretty liberally, muck has a habit of sneaking up on you. Much better to spend a little longer and get the whole thing clean.

Well, they often are like that!

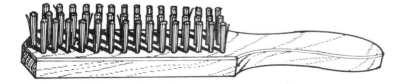

Wire brush

Scrape the worst off first

When you have got the obvious bulk dirt off, paying particular attention to flanges and around fastenings, then start wiping down with old newspaper. It is absorbent and cheap, and readily available. To finish the job off, get an old paintbrush, dip it in paraffin and wipe the surface clean.

A very useful de-greasing agent is sold under the trade name of 'Gunk'. This can be simply brushed onto a greasy and dirty surface, left for a few minutes and then washed off with water, taking all the dirt with it in an oily emulsion. Be careful about polluting your drains if you use this technique. Before washing, cover the air intake, ignition coil and distributor with plastic bags. Never use water or paraffin on a hot engine.

Opening up

Before separating any sealed joint, be sure that the surrounding area is quite clean. Once you have exposed the 'works' in any way, be careful no dirt gets in. It can be knocked off other adjacent surfaces, can fall from the ceiling of your garage, or even blow in from outside through an open door. Keep components covered when you are not working on them.

Be careful where you put things down

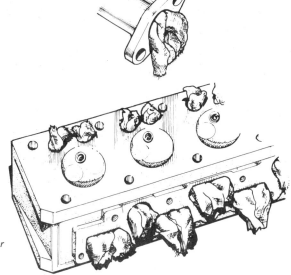

Plug openings with rag or paper

Cavities which would be difficult to clean should be temporarily plugged while you are working near them. Particular examples are fuel pipes, oil pipes, and cooling water and oil passages in cylinder head and block. A twist of rag or paper tucked in the hole is probably most suitable. Make them big enough not to be forgotten about or pushed through into the cavity.

Even workbench surfaces are likely to be dirty. Cover with clean newspaper before laying components out. The paper absorbs oil drips and can quickly be changed when it gets dirty. Keep any exposed steel surfaces lubricated to avoid rust.

Fine cleaning

Paper towels or tissues are suitable for wiping finished surfaces. Soaking components in paraffin or petrol is the traditional way of getting them really clean. Components which have been subjected to wear and have been running in hot oil very often tend to build up a surface film from impurities in the oil. A good long soaking in petrol followed by brushing with a stiff nylon brush will help to remove this film. Gaskets and joint surfaces which have had jointing compound on them can be cleaned with methylated spirit or petrol.

Soak in kerosene or petrol for cleaning

The inside of oil passageways, sumps, camshaft covers, etc tends to get coated with a fine sludge deposited from the oil. This should be removed with newspaper, followed by paraffin or a degreaser. Apart from the fact that it is aesthetically unpleasant for you to handle, some of this slime will contaminate the new oil you put in afterwards.

Hand cleaning

Inevitably your hands, at least, will get dirty, if not other parts of you. An antiseptic barrier cream rubbed into the skin of your hands **before** you start will reduce the danger of infection and will ease the subsequent cleansing process. For this you will need a combination of degreasing agent and abrasive. Special hand cleaners such as 'Swarfega' can be purchased which combine both features. Alternatives are the use of a degreaser, such as 'Gunk' or soft soap backed up with a stiff brush or scouring pad (ouch!), or one of the domestic scouring powders such as 'Vim' or 'White Tide'.

Basic principles

Whenever two surfaces are rubbed against each other you get 'friction' which opposes the movement. This is caused because the surfaces are never really smooth. Magnified greatly, any material surface looks like a picture of the Alps, and the facing 'mountain peaks' on the two surfaces interlock. As the two faces are moved relative to each other, these peaks are sheared off.

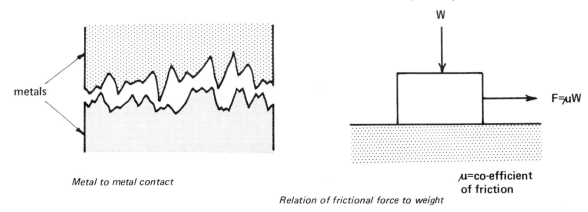

Metal to metal contact

Relation of frictional force to weight

The force required to do this is the frictional force, which is proportional to the pressure squeezing the faces together and the 'coefficient of friction' of the materials. The energy required to overcome the frictional force causes heating of the rubbing surfaces and can be enough to heat metal to melting point, resulting in the surfaces welding together.

In any piece of engineering equipment it is necessary for surfaces to move relative to each other continually, with the minimum of wear, and the design of these 'bearings' is a complex subject. There are a number of ways of minimising the frictional loss in a bearing (and hence the rate of wear). An obvious starting point is to keep the relative speed and the pressure on the bearing low, and this indeed was the saviour of the ancient windmills and water-mills. It is not very practicable for high power machinery, and a logical further development was to choose

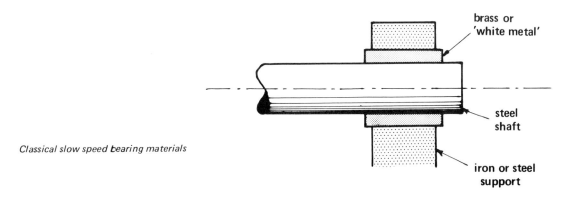

Classical slow speed bearing materials

bearing materials which have a low coefficient of friction. Cast iron and brass make good partners and were to be found in many early machines, to be refined later into steel rubbing against 'white metal' or 'Babbitt' (a tin alloy). Many modern bearings take advantage of the low coefficient of friction of some of the plastics such as 'Tufnol', nylon and PTFE (poly-tetra-fluor-ethylene).

However, the method which has dominated most bearing design has been to keep the bearing surfaces apart with a material which has both a low coefficient of friction and a low shear strength. The effort then is expended in moving this 'lubricant' relative to itself and the main surfaces are not in contact. Of course, if the film of lubricant does break down and you get metal to metal contact, it is usually followed by extremely rapid wear.

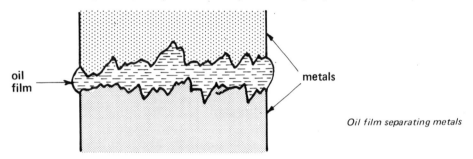

oil film → ← metals

Oil film separating metals

In relatively lightly loaded bearings it is sufficient to provide an initial lubricant film which is replenished rarely, if at all. More heavily loaded ones require regular or continuous lubrication and the heaviest loads require forced high lubricant pressures to maintain the film.

Types of lubricant

Oil

The basic lubricants you will need to concern yourself with are the petroleum oils. These are distilled from the same crude oils which provide petrol, paraffin, diesel and fuel oils. Many different types are blended to meet the needs of different industries. Motor oils, although marketed now by many firms, are fairly well standardised; differing only marginally in their properties.

The oils you will need most of are the main engine lubricants. These are usually distinguished by their viscosity ratings. The viscosity is the 'runniness' of the oil. You need an oil which stays fluid at low temperatures to ensure good lubrication and easy starting on winter mornings, and yet it must not become too runny and thin at high engine temperatures. The viscosity is measured in a standard manner and awarded a rating number in accordance with standards laid down by the American Society of Automobile Engineers (SAE). Some oils, known as multi-grade oils, behave in a different manner at low and high temperatures, and these are indicated by dual rating numbers, eg SAE 20/50. Your vehicle handbook will tell you what grade of oil to use. Do as it says; the designers know more about it than you do.

Engine oil is always a compromise. It is exposed to high temperatures, acid deposits and water from the combustion chamber; it has to lubricate the sliding piston surfaces, the very heavily loaded crankshaft bearings, the high temperature valve guides, and has to act as a supplementary engine coolant. Under these conditions it is not surprising that it tends to decompose and needs regular replacement.

Away from the engine, the designer has greater opportunity to refine his lubricants, and it is usual practice to find a special gear oil specified for the gearbox. This will be chosen to reduce to a minimum the frictional losses in the gearbox to improve efficiency, while still obtaining a long oil life. Further back still you are likely to find a 'hypoid' oil specified for the rear axle gears. This oil is specially designed to withstand the very high pressure sliding loads occurring in the 'spiral hypoid' right angle drive commonly employed in automobiles.

You will also need a light 'machine oil' for miscellaneous lubrication of lightly loaded bearings, eg throttle linkages.

Grease

The blending of higher viscosity oils with 'soaps' produces greases. These can vary from little thicker than oil to almost a wax-like consistency. They are generally applied where high bearing pressures must be withstood without regular replenishment. Once a film of grease is formed in a bearing, it is more tenacious than oil. The two common uses you will meet are for the lubrication of ball and roller bearings (eg wheel hubs), and where there are small, high-load movements (eg suspension joints).

On older vehicles it was usual for provision to be made for forcing new grease in to replace old lubricant. Grease 'nipples' would be provided, which lead via a passage to the bearing surface. Grease is pumped in through the nipple under very high pressure until the old grease is squeezed out of the edge of the bearing. To provide the necessary pressure you require a 'grease gun'. The high quality type has a nozzle, on one end of a short hose pipe, which clips onto the grease

Grease nipple

Grease gun

nipple. The other end of the hose is connected to a lever operated pump mounted on a grease container. The simpler type of grease gun has a rigid nozzle which is spring loaded in the grease container. The nozzle is placed against the nipple and the container forced forward against the spring. This action holds the nozzle firmly on the nipple and at the same time pumps a small quantity of grease out.

Dry lubricants

These materials act in a slightly different manner to the normal lubricant. Applied to a metal surface, they form a molecular bond with that surface and give it the coefficient of friction of the lubricant. The bearing action is therefore relative movement of surfaces of the lubricant. The oldest known is graphite, a form of carbon, which has a molecular structure of thin overlapping plates which slide very easily over each other. A more recent innovation is molybdenum-disulphide which has better surface bonding characteristics.

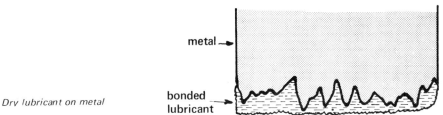

metal →

bonded
lubricant →

Dry lubricant on metal

Graphite can be obtained as a dry powder or as a colloidal suspension in water or oil. The use of the dry or water carried forms is very suitable for high temperature components such as nuts on exhaust fittings. It will maintain its lubricating properties where oil would just burn off, leaving a sticky residue. Molybdenum-disulphide is similarly available in several forms. The oil suspensions of graphite or molybdenum-disulphide are very useful additives for engine oil. They give a marginal reduction in friction until the oil is changed, but more importantly they build up a protective layer on the bearing surfaces. This reduces wear at cold starts and gives protection in the event of oil pressure failure. For an advertising stunt on one occasion, molybdenum-disulphide was added to the engine oil of a small automobile. It was then driven about 200 miles to thoroughly circulate the additive, the engine oil was drained, and then the vehicle was driven the 200 miles back, relying only on the deposited film of molybdenum-disulphide. This was achieved without engine failure, but is hardly recommended for normal use.

Bearing lubrication

There are a number of different types of bearing which you will encounter in your vehicle, each with its own lubrication system.

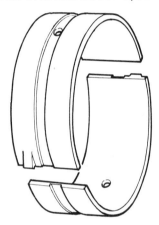

Bearing 'shells'

Main journal bearings

These are the main engine bearings in which the crankshaft rotates, and on the ends of the connecting rods (the big end bearings). The shaft has a highly polished and hardened steel surface and rotates in a 'white metal' shell. These 'shell' bearings consist of thin semi-circular strips of steel coated on one face with a low coefficient of friction metal. A pair of shells, forming a complete circle, are supported and clamped in a forged steel housing. Lubrication of the bearings is by oil forced in at high pressure by a pump. Similar bearings are also to be found on camshafts and other auxiliary drives.

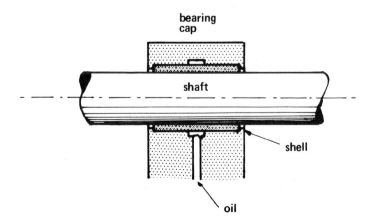

Section through assembled shell bearing

Pistons

The pistons sliding in the cylinders perform on high speed heavily loaded bearings. They are lubricated by the sprayed oil coming from the edges of the big end and main bearings.

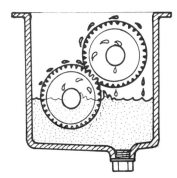

Gear lubrication

Gears

The meshing faces of the gears have a combined rolling and sliding bearing action. They are usually lubricated by arranging for part of the gear train to dip into an oil bath. The gear teeth themselves then act as a pump to keep the bearing surface supplied with lubricant.

Sleeve bearings

Some shaft bearings with only medium speed and load requirements are provided with a steel bearing surface running in a 'sintered bronze' sleeve. This material is formed in such a manner that it has a micro-porous surface which will absorb and retain oil. Once impregnated, the bearing will run for a long time without attention. For high temperature use, the bronze sleeve is sometimes impregnated with graphite. This type of bearing has replaced many of the grease lubricated suspension joints used on older cars, allowing bearings to be sealed for the life of the vehicles. In yet other cases a rubber bush has replaced altogether the metal to metal bearing. Relative movement of the joint components is then obtained by the flexing of the rubber without sliding friction.

Ball bearing

Ball and roller bearings

In this type of bearing, sliding movement is replaced by rolling, with its much lower frictional losses. The components of the bearing must be extremely hard to withstand the very high point loads on the balls or rollers, and a very high finish is required. As a result, this type of bearing is expensive. It is primarily used for wheel bearings which would be difficult to lubricate if any other type were used and where low frictional losses are important. Lubrication is normally by packing the bearing and its housing with grease. Sometimes bearings of this type are sealed and require no further lubrication during their life.

Lubrication practice

Bright spots and stains on bearing surfaces usually indicate where wear is taking place. If these are not uniformly distributed over the bearing surface, there may be some distortion or misalignment which requires correction. Look particularly for 'scuffing', where a bearing surface has been roughened. This indicates partial breakdown of the lubrication film, resulting in metal to metal contact. Failure will eventually result.

All bearing surfaces should be given a film of lubricant as they are assembled. It may take some time for the normal lubrication method to become re-established once running starts again. Lubricate all threads before assembly; high temperature ones with graphite. It will make dismantling next time much easier. A dab of grease can be used for holding small components in place while you are assembling, with no subsequent deleterious effect. This is particularly relevant with needle roller and small ball bearings. Do not pack too much grease into ball or roller bearings; the grease will melt into the bearing as it is required.

If you are going to store bare steel components, coat them with a film of grease to prevent rusting.

To prevent the lubricant working out of the bearing and contaminating other parts of the vehicle, oil seals are usually fitted where shafts leave an enclosure. Usually made of synthetic rubber, they must be very carefully assembled to avoid creasing or damaging the sealing face.

It may perhaps be stating the obvious, but before you can take something apart, you first have to identify the joints and the method of fastening employed. For parts of the vehicle which are disguised by the decorative trim, this can often be a time consuming exercise. Look for screws disguised as decoration or accessible from underneath or behind a component. If all else fails, see if the trim will just spring off. Usually the main fastenings are then obvious.

Fastening hidden by trim   *Mixed fastenings on joint*

Although in most cases one set of fastenings of the same type will hold together one joint, sometimes there will be more than one type of fastening used and sometimes more than one joint held by the same fastening. For example, you may find a flanged joint held on three sides by nuts and bolts but on the fourth side screws have been used because there was no space for through bolt holes. You will often find brake drums held in position by one or two countersunk screws. These however are only a convenience; the main fastening comes when the wheel is secured over the brake drum by its own nuts.

Recording

Before separating any joint, check if it is possible to re-assemble it in a different position. If so, scribe a clear mark across the joint line so that you can be sure that you replace it in the correct position. If you are disconnecting hosepipes or wires, fix a label of some sort — a tie-on tag or a piece of paper covered by clear adhesive tape — to each beforehand and make a simple sketch of the connection positions.

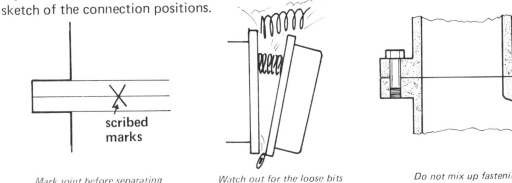

Mark joint before separating   *Watch out for the loose bits*   *Do not mix up fastenings*

When you open something up, watch out for washers, springs, gaskets and small components which may fall out. Keep components together with their own fastenings in some sort of container, eg an egg box for nuts, bolts and washers. If there is any possibility of confusion, keep a record. For example, two screws may be the same diameter but one may be ¼ inch longer than the other. Replacing the long screw in a blind hole meant for the shorter screw will prevent you from tightening up properly.

Undoing fastenings

Nuts, bolts, screws and other fastenings which have been exposed to corrosion can sometimes be very difficult to release. Clean any dirt and rust away before you start so that you can see what you are doing. If it looks as if things are going to be tight, a good squirt of 'penetrating oil' (also called 'easing oil') will do wonders. This is a special blend of oil with a very low viscosity which will soak into the tiniest crevice. Its lubricating properties are not very wonderful but they can make all the difference to a tight screw.

If you have to hit the threaded end of a bolt to free it, always screw a nut on flush with the end of the bolt so that the threads are not damaged. Use a rubber or copper mallet, or interpose a block of hardwood between the hammer and the bolt.

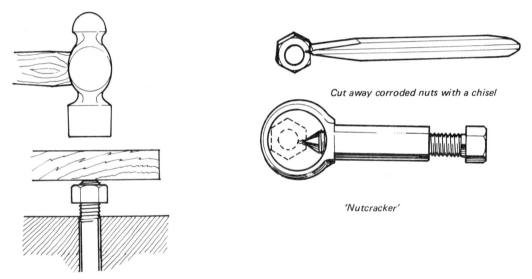

Cut away corroded nuts with a chisel

'Nutcracker'

Never hit directly on the end of a bolt

Occasionally a nut may be so badly corroded that it has to be cut away. A blow with a cold chisel on one of the nut faces can split the nut and allow it to be removed. If you expect to be faced with this problem often (you are rebuilding an old banger perhaps), you can buy a tool known as a 'nut-cracker'. A forging encircles the nut and a screw can be tightened up to force a chisel inwards to split it.

If a bolt or fitting is very tight, the application of localised heat from a blow-lamp or similar

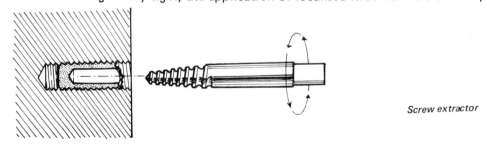

Screw extractor

source can sometimes give enough slack to help. However, if this technique is to be tried, be very careful! Make sure that there is nothing nearby which can be set on fire, and also that the component concerned is not a heat-treated item which will have its strength impaired if it is heated.

If a screw shears off, leaving the broken end still in the threaded hole, it can be removed with a screw extractor, sometimes called an 'easi-out'. This looks rather like an oversize woodscrew with a left hand thread. A hole is drilled in the broken screw and the extractor screwed into this hole. Now, the more force required to turn the screw, the more the extractor grips it.

Separating a joint

Separating joints

When you have removed all the fastenings the joint should come apart easily. However, a sealing compound may have been used, in which case a good thump with a soft faced mallet is needed. Alternatively, a blow with a hammer on a block of hardwood may be capable of being better directed. Apply the force to something which can withstand the blow, not some minor protruberance, such as a pipe or stud, which could be damaged.

If the components of the joint move, but still do not want to come apart, have another good look. The chances are that there is another fastening somewhere that you have missed.

Carefully save any gasket if it is possible to do so. It may come in useful as an emergency spare in the future, even if you are not going to re-use it immediately.

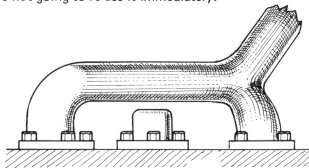

The correct assembly sequence is important

Putting it together

When you come to reassemble all the bits, be sure that you quite clearly understand the sequence of assembly. Quite often you will find that you cannot obtain access to component 'A' once component 'B' has been fitted. The fitting of spring and plain washers and split pins can easily be forgotten. Before fastening a cover on, have a last look through the box of components to see if there are any more bits which should be under this cover before you screw it down. It can be very frustrating if you have spent a lot of time bedding in a gasket and tightening down perhaps twenty screws, to find a vital locking plate left out.

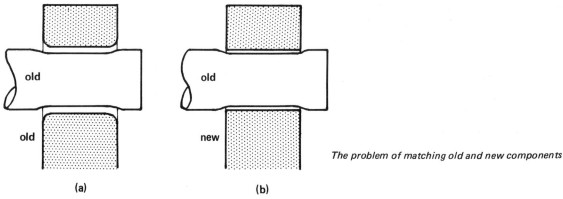

The problem of matching old and new components

(a)   (b)

Checking new components

If you are fitting new components make sure that they are the correct pattern. Compare them carefully with the old components, and offer them up to check if they will fit in their proper place. Where there are wearing surfaces, eg bearings, it will sometimes be necessary to change both components. The old components will have worn to match each other and may work adequately; one worn and one new component may be quite incompatible.

Make sure that protective films and plugs are removed from new components, otherwise you may have some rather odd results.

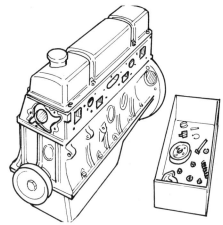

Make sure no bits are left out

Assembly

When refitting existing components, make sure that the location marks line up; ie the component goes back exactly where it was before. Do not force or strain unless the instruction book specifies a tight fit.

All movable connections should be lubricated before assembly and tested for free movement before tightening fastenings. The movement should be checked again after securing the fastenings. If things have tightened up significantly, then something is being distorted by the fastenings. Check for dirt on a location face, bearing misalignment or bent components.

So, you have now finished putting everything back together. What are those two washers, one spring and that piece of pipe doing lying in the components box? Did you really mean to leave them out or did you just forget them?

The chances are that by the time you finish, you are tired and cold and your tea is waiting. There is a temptation to shut the lid, clean up your hands and leave the vehicle, assuming that everything is now all right. If you do, the law of perversity guarantees that you will have done something wrong, and when you go to drive off in a hurry the following day, it will not work. You **must** spend that extra time to check that everything you have disturbed (and that means **everything**) will work correctly.

Anti-corrosion protection

It has already been said that steel will corrode very rapidly if exposed to damp air. Other materials oxidise more slowly. The first line of attack against corrosion is to stop it happening in the first place. This means ensuring that bare steel is never exposed. Any cut edges should be protected with paint immediately, and the vehicle's basic paintwork should be carefully checked for defects. High speed, low cost production always gives the risk of skimped work. Look particularly at joints between the body panels and at the under surfaces. If any of the paint looks a bit thin, give it another coat.

Modern automobile finishing usually consists of an 'etching' primer first. This bonds onto the clean metal surface and provides a base for further coats of paint. There will be one or more coats of undercoat paint followed by the finishing top coat. It is common practice to coat the underbody of the vehicle with a very thick bituminous coating ('underseal'), which protects the metalwork from erosion by stones, grit and road salt.

Touching up

The paintwork of an automobile is vulnerable to chipping by flying stones, particularly the front and lower side panels. These chip marks should not be left as they represent weaknesses in the paint where corrosion can start. Indeed in some cases the chip may penetrate right through to the metal, resulting in a rust spot forming.

Touch-up paints are available to match the specific colours of most current models and many older ones. They are available in either a 'pen' form or a small tin with a brush attached to the lid. With a piece of sandpaper or emery cloth, remove any traces of rust and roughen the paint surface in the immediate vicinity (say 1/8 inch to 1/4 inch) of a chip mark. Then dab on the touch-up paint to fill up the chip mark and overlap onto the surrounding paint.

Painting larger areas

If you have to paint a larger area, you will have to give a little more thought to the paint to be used. Automobile paintwork generally is carried out with paint which is dried rapidly in an oven. For many paints this is an irreversible process, but there are some thermoplastic ('Heat-flowed') paints which will soften again if exposed to heat.

The vehicle manufacturer or paint manufacturers are usually willing to recommend suitable paints for repair jobs which are compatible with the original paint. A very fast drying paint has the advantage of not being so vulnerable to blown dust during the drying period, but requires skill to get it on smoothly with a brush before it stiffens.

Spraying the paint on obviously avoids this problem but gives others instead. In the handy aerosol spray packs the paint is rather expensive and it needs a number of coats to thoroughly cover the work. There is also the problem of adequately masking the area to be painted, so that you do not spray everything else in the neighbourhood. Mist from a paint spray can drift quite a way, so be careful.

If you use a slower drying paint, make sure that you take precautions to exclude dust.

Drying can be accelerated by exposing the paint to heat from special infra-red electric lamps.

Matching the existing paintwork may prove a problem. Paint continually changes its colour with age, and even if your new patch matches correctly when applied, the differing ageing rates may give a mis-match in a year's time.

Surface preparation

Assuming you are repainting after repairing some damage. First you must ensure that the base metal is smooth. A sanding disc fitted to an electric drill can be of help for this hard-work stage. Small ripples can be very difficult to remove, and the answer here is a 'stopper/filler'. This is a priming paint containing a high proportion of solid material. It leaves a thick film which fills the valleys and can be rubbed down to give a smooth blend into the finished surface. In any case a primer paint is needed for use on bare metal.

The treatment is then successive coats of paint, rubbed down with successively finer grades of abrasive paper until the finish is smooth enough to take the final gloss coat. This should be allowed to harden for several days before finally polishing.

Make sure that all traces of rust are removed before starting to paint. This is particularly important for crevices and joints in panels. Proprietary solvents are available which will chemically remove the last traces of rust, after the wire brush and emery cloth have removed the bulk. These solvents will also etch the metal to give a better bond for the priming coat.

Glass fibre patches

For repairing badly corroded areas, or where you wish to change the shape of a panel, you will need that useful material, glass reinforced plastic (GRP), commonly called glass fibre or fibre-glass.

This consists of a resin and hardener mixture which, like the epoxy adhesive described earlier, starts a chemical reaction as soon as mixed, together with a mat of chopped up glass fibres. The mat is impregnated with the resin, and when the resin has hardened you are left with a strong and light structural material.

The proportions of resin and hardener will vary according to the materials used, and it is advisable for you to buy one of the readily available repair kits which give full instructions for applying the matched sets of glass mats, resin and hardener.

Before using a glass fibre patch, make sure that you have removed all traces of rust in the area and cut back the corroded metal to the point where it is nearly at full strength.

Lifting heavy weights is a job you will be faced with from time to time. It is an operation fraught with danger, both to you and to the machinery, and should be undertaken with great care, using the right tools. This is one place where you must never be prepared to settle for second best.

Typical car jack

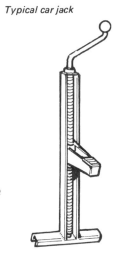

The vehicle jack

The most common lift you will need to make is one using the jack supplied with the vehicle. With modern automobiles this is a rather flimsy screw operated device which locates into sockets in the vehicle frame.

If you have any choice in the matter, make sure that the vehicle is on level ground before attempting to jack it up. Apply the handbrake firmly, unless you are going to need to turn the wheels after lifting. In any case, place rocks or other wedges in front of and behind the wheels which will stay firmly on the ground. This will all help to keep the vehicle in one place, as the vehicle jack is usually lacking in any significant sidewards stability. Unless the jack will rest on a very hard surface, place a thick piece of timber or a metal plate under the foot of the jack to

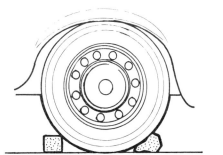

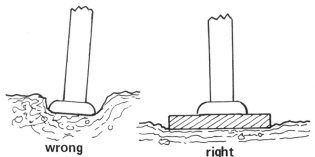

Always wedge the wheels before jacking   *Spread the load under the foot of the jack*

spread the load. A heavy automobile supported on a narrow jack face can force it down even into a tarmac surface.

Make sure that the lifting lug on the jack is inserted completely into the socket on the vehicle. If it is only partly inserted there is a tendency to bend the lug and distort the vehicle frame. Because of the positioning of the sockets on some vehicles, they tend to collect mud and gravel. This must be cleared out before attempting to insert the jack.

Never rely on just the vehicle jack if you are going to do much work, particularly if you need to get underneath the vehicle. Build up a supporting pillar of wooden blocks to act as a back-up.

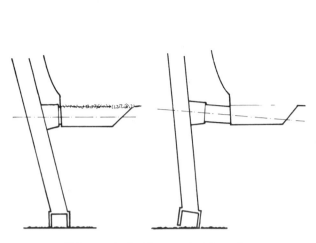

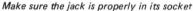

Make sure the jack is properly in its socket

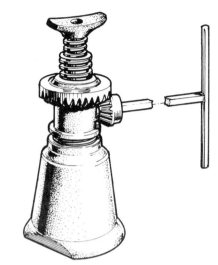

General purpose screw jack

Other jacks

In garages it is normal practice to use separate universal jacks, and many older automobiles were supplied with one which did not depend upon particular locations on the vehicle. You may decide that such a universal jack may be of value to you. The big, high lift, hydraulic, trolley jack used in garages is far too expensive for home use, but smaller versions are now available. Some can be very flimsy, so be careful that you get one certified as capable of lifting at least two-thirds of your vehicle's weight. More commonly available are simple upright screw or hydraulic jacks. In general these tend to be more robust.

These separate jacks usually have a slightly dished lifting pad on top. This must be located on a part of the vehicle capable of taking the load. The general tin-ware parts of a modern automobile are invariably **not** suitable for this purpose; they will just crumple up if you try to lift under them. The traditional points used by garage staff, apart from designed jacking points, are under the front suspension frame, the back axle or the clutch housing mounting.

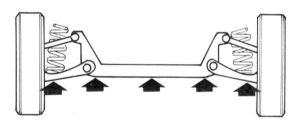

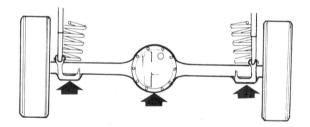

Safe lifting points

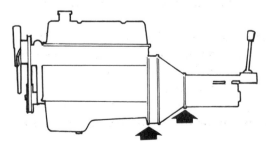

Ramps and stands

A useful adjunct for routine under-vehicle maintenance is a pair of steel ramps. These are robust frames with an incline at one end up which the vehicle can be driven, to give a lift of about a foot. Although much safer than jacks, you still should not ignore the precaution of wedging the wheels to prevent movement.

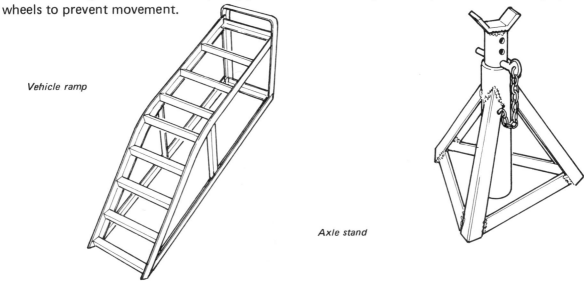

Vehicle ramp

Axle stand

Major vehicle work, requiring the removal of two or more wheels, needs the use of supporting stands. Strong base frames have telescopic extensions which can be locked in a number of positions. A corner of the vehicle is jacked up and a stand adjusted to locate on a suitable chassis member. As the jack is lowered again, the stand takes the weight and the jack can be moved to another position.

Levers

The basic mechanical principle of the lever is one you should study, as its application can be very useful. The lever is a strong bar of metal or wood which will not bend or break under the load which you wish to lift. The lever is rested on a 'fulcrum', a solid object on which the lever can rock. There are two forms of lever which are relevant to lifting heavy loads. In one, the load is at one end and the force to lift it is applied at the other end, with the fulcrum in between; in the second form the fulcrum is at one end, the load near to the fulcrum, and the lift at the

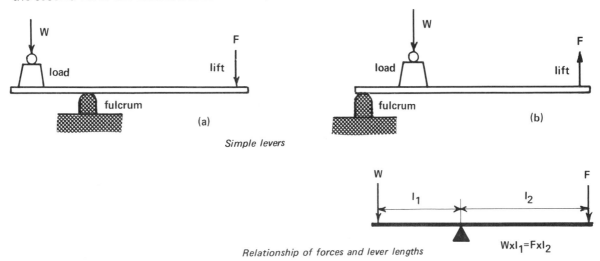

Simple levers

Relationship of forces and lever lengths $W \times l_1 = F \times l_2$

opposite end. In both cases, the load multiplied by its distance to the fulcrum is always equal to the lifting force multiplied by **its** distance to the fulcrum. So, the nearer the load is to the fulcrum, the less force you need to lift it. With a suitable strong lever and the correct positioning of the fulcrum, an average strength person can lift more than a ton. There is a snag however — the distance moved is inversely proportional to the relative forces. For example, if a lever arm ratio of 10 to 1 is made, you can lift 500 pounds by exerting a force of only 50 pounds, but a movement of your hands of 20 inches will raise the load only 2 inches.

A very efficient application of the lever principle is the crow-bar, pry-bar or 'jemmy'. This is a strong steel bar, one end of which is forged into a wedge-shaped tongue (often forked) with a curved base. The wedge tip can be rammed into a small crevice beneath a heavy object and the bar then rocked on the curved base as the fulcrum. The curvature is usually such that the initial leverage is very high.

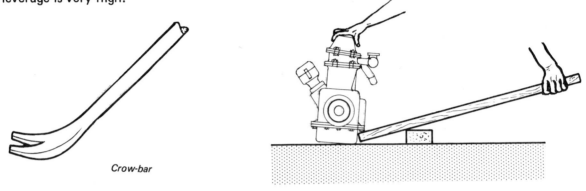

Crow-bar

Using a simple lever to move a heavy weight

However, even without this refinement, a lot can be done with blocks of wood and steel bars. If you have to move a heavy weight slightly, it is always worth trying to set up a simple lever rather than struggle with a direct hand lift. You will have much more control. Make sure that you apply your lifting force to a part of the machinery that can take the weight.

Hoists

As already indicated, one of the biggest snags with the lever is its limited lift. A development of the lever principle which overcomes this problem is the pulley block hoist. Let us see how this development works in practice.

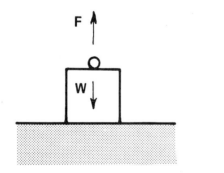

Straight lift

To lift a heavy load upwards may be just too much of a strain for one person. However, using his weight that person could probably easily exert that amount of force downwards. So, a logical action is to fasten a rope to the load, take it upwards over a pulley which is secured to a roof beam, and then it is ready to take the downward pull. The force (F) on the end of the rope

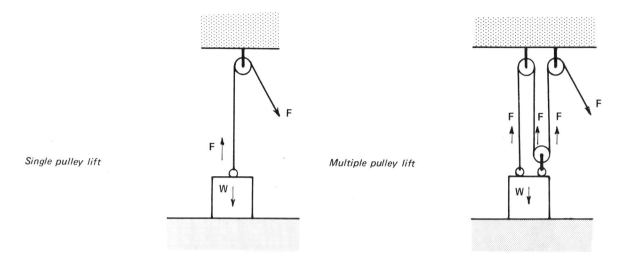

Single pulley lift   *Multiple pulley lift*

is obviously the same as the weight (W) being lifted.

If the rope is now taken around another pulley fastened to the load, and back up over another fastened to the beam, it can be seen that the same force (F) appears in three ropes leading from the load. The weight can therefore be equal to three times the pull on the end of the rope. However, like the lever, you do not get something for nothing, and the movement of the end of the rope is three times the movement of the load. This is not usually much of a problem; you just need a good long rope.

The number of pulleys and strands of rope can be multiplied almost indefinitely to obtain enormous leverage. There are now available on the market some very neat, compact hoists with nylon rope which are marketed especially for the do-it-yourself automobilist, and have a lifting capacity of up to two tons.

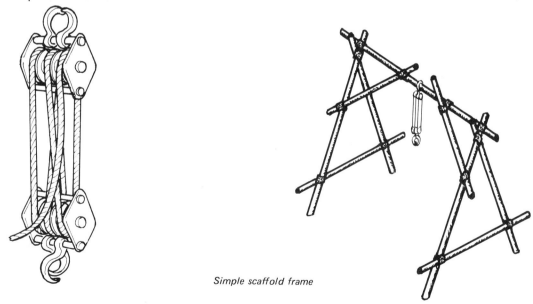

Simple scaffold frame

Make sure that the beam to which you anchor your hoist is strong enough to take the load you intend to lift. The light wooden rafters often used in suburban garage construction are probably not. A simple frame can easily be made up from scaffold tubing which will straddle your vehicle and be strong enough to take the weight of the engine. The tubing and fittings can be bought fairly cheaply, or rented for even less.

Slinging

Reference has so far been made simply to 'lifting the load'. However, the art of 'slinging', attaching the load to the hoist or lever, can be quite tricky. The 'slings' are usually wire, hemp or nylon rope. Commercial slings are spliced in a loop and are tested and certified for a particular maximum load. You will usually be just lashing something up for the job. Always allow more strands than you think you will need; make sure that they can move freely through the hoist hook, so that they can share the load properly. Be careful of the knots you use, particularly with nylon rope which is so smooth that a knot can be pulled undone sometimes. Try to arrange the slings so that the knots are not directly loaded.

Pick anchor points for lifting which are likely to stand the strain. Some engines and other heavy components are provided with proper lifting eyes. Never let the 'legs' of a sling spread to more than a 60° angle; the strength of the sling drops very rapidly beyond this point.

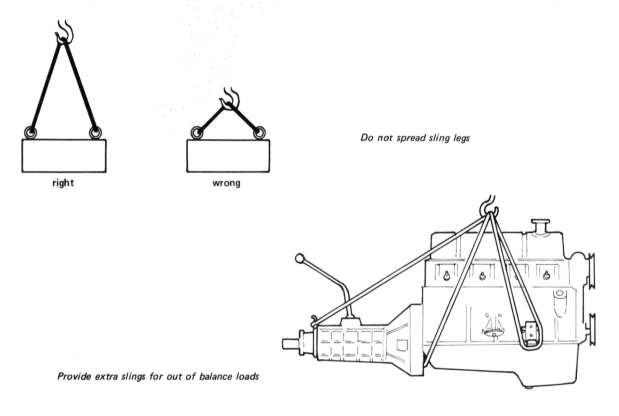

right   wrong

Do not spread sling legs

Provide extra slings for out of balance loads

Give some thought to where the centre of gravity is (where the bulk of the weight is) before you start to lift. The item may tilt and cause slings to slip. An extra, balancing sling may be necessary.

When starting a lift, take up the slack in the slings and then lift the load slightly and lower again. Check the slings for security again before carrying on with the lift.

Now that we have come nearly to the end of the book, it seems to be an appropriate moment to consider how some of the rules and tools which have been described are applied in practice. Two common beginner's jobs are described in detail — fitting a pair of reversing lights and replacing a corroded silencer.

Job 1 — Reversing lights

Planning

Firstly, you examine the lamps available on the market and decide that a pair of flush mounted ones with 24 watt bulbs are appropriate to the styling of the vehicle; you also decide that as you will have to mount an auxiliary panel to carry the switch and pilot lamp, you will provide switches for the future fitting of a fog lamp and a spot lamp while you are about it. Lamps of that type will probably have 48 or 60 watt bulbs in them. Starting with this basic information you must first draw yourself a circuit diagram. By the way, it is a legal requirement that a reversing lamp controlled by a separate switch must have a pilot lamp adjacent to the switch to warn when it is on; it is also good practice to provide pilot lamps for the fog and spot lamps as well.

The power supply would be best taken from the circuit which is controlled by the ignition switch, then the lamps cannot be left on by accident. A connection needs to be made from the supply to the three switches (reversing, fog and spot) in parallel. From the opposite side of each switch, a pilot lamp will be connected to earth (the frame) so that the pilot lamp lights if the switch is operated. From the reversing light switch a wire must run to the back of the vehicle to connect to the two lamps in parallel which will be earthed on the other side to complete the circuit.

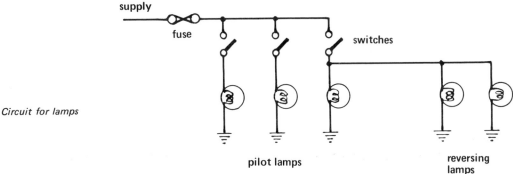

Circuit for lamps

Now, each reversing lamp is 24 watts so that at 12 volts it requires 2 amps of current (2 x 12 =24). The cable connecting the second lamp will carry only 2 amps and could in theory be smaller than the cable feeding the two lamps together which will carry 4 amps. You would not of course in practice bother to buy a few feet of smaller cable but make it all the larger size. From the table in Chapter 19 it will be seen that a 14/.010 cable will be an adequate size to carry 4 amps. However, for the feed cable to the switch panel, there will also be the heavier current for the future fog and spot lamps. If they are 48 watt lamps, they will draw 4 amps each (4 x 12 = 48), a total of 12 amps including the 4 amps for the reversing lights. If the main lamps are 60 watt rating, the total current would be 14 amps. In either case, 28/.012 cable will be adequate for the load.

The next stage is to check the vehicle wiring diagram in the service manual. Some manufacturers make provision in the initial vehicle wiring for future auxiliaries, so this must first be looked for. On the practical wiring diagram you spot a connector left sticking out of the wiring harness adjacent to the rear lights; this could be it. But checking back the wire colours shows that this is simply connected to the side/tail light circuit as provision for a boot interior illumination lamp. There is, after all, no alternative to running in new cable. The cable to the reversing lamps should be green with another trace colour, to fit the scheme described in Chapter 19. Examination of the wiring diagram shows that green/red is an acceptable colour for this circuit and the supply cable must be green. The manufacturer has already provided a 16 amp fuse ready for the connection of auxiliary circuits which are to be ignition switch controlled.

The final part of the planning process is to actually trace through the circuit, step by step, on the vehicle to check the way in which it will be installed. Firstly, the supply fuse has a plain connection blade, so a push-on cable connector will be needed. The cable can run alongside the main wiring harness to the point where it passes through the bulkhead, from the engine compartment to the driving compartment. At this point there is a large rubber grommet, or protective bushing, for the harness. Careful probing shows that another cable could be worked through the grommet.

Now, where to mount the switch panel? There is an obvious place at the bottom of the instrument panel, to the left of the steering column, with the metal panel turned back to form a flange underneath. Any cable connectors required on the switch panel can be finalised only when the switches and pilot lamps have been chosen, but they will probably be push-on ones again.

The cable run to the rear of the vehicle is the next point to be checked, and here there is a snag. The main wiring harness feeding the stop and tail lights is run through a hollow frame member up the side of the windscreen and above the doors. A bit of probing shows that the chances of threading another cable by this route are pretty slim, so some other route must be pioneered. Underneath the carpeting, embedded in the sound absorption felt, seems to offer good prospects, and this can be followed right through, except for the bulkhead between the rear passenger seat and the boot. This will require to be drilled to pass the cable through, and that means adding a protective grommet to the shopping list.

Finally, there is a clear flat area at the back where cut-outs can be made for mounting the reversing lamps themselves. For both the lamps and the switch panel, self-tapping screws seem to be the most likely fixing method. An estimate is made of the lengths of cable which will be required.

Shopping

Now that the planning stage is complete, you can draw up your shopping list:

2	—	flush mounting, 24 watt reversing lamps
	—	self-tapping screws for fixing lamps
1	—	switch and lamp panel
	—	self-tapping screws for fixing switch panel
3	—	switches
2	—	blue pilot lights (for fog and spot lamps)

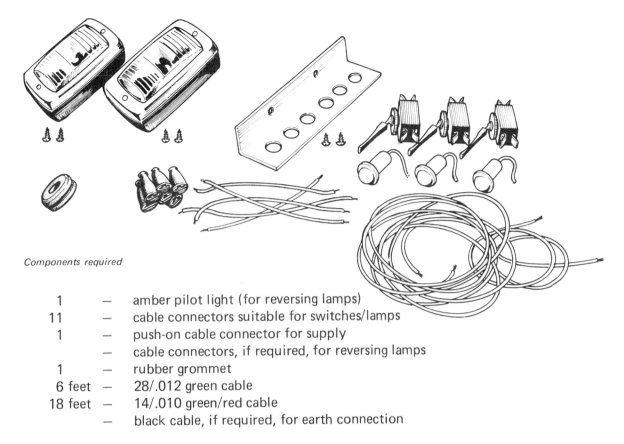

Components required

1	—	amber pilot light (for reversing lamps)
11	—	cable connectors suitable for switches/lamps
1	—	push-on cable connector for supply
	—	cable connectors, if required, for reversing lamps
1	—	rubber grommet
6 feet	—	28/.012 green cable
18 feet	—	14/.010 green/red cable
	—	black cable, if required, for earth connection

A visit to your local do-it-yourself 'speed shop' produces all the necessary bits. As expected, the reversing lamps have screw terminals for the supply lead and do not need cable connectors, and the earth connection is made through the lamp housing. The switches need push-on connectors, but the pilot lamps are earthed to the frame on one side and have a short lead already attached to the other side. A suitable auxiliary switch panel is available already painted and with six holes of the right size to take the switches and pilot lamps. The switch panel and the reversing lamps each need two fixing screws, all of the same size. A quick mental check confirms that your tool kit contains a suitable size drill for the self-tapping screws.

Fitting

The first job to be done when you return from your shopping is to offer up the reversing lamps and the switch panel, to confirm that they **do** look all right where you planned them, and to lay out the cable to be sure that you really did allow enough spare.

Marking out for reversing lamp

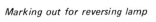

Then mark out the position for the reversing lamps. Fix the centre line of one relative to some existing fitting, say, the fastenings of the tail light; follow this with the same dimensions for the other one on the opposite side. Mark out for each, the centres for the fixing holes and the outline of the cut-out to be made. You have decided to use the drill and file method of cutting the large holes, and the next stage is to scribe in the lines for the rows of holes to be drilled. Centre-pops are made for the fixing holes, to identify the edges of the cut-out and for every one of the small holes.

At this stage adhesive tape is stuck on to protect the paintwork in the immediate vicinity of the cutting, and newspaper placed in the boot to catch metal fragments. A 3/16 inch diameter drill bit has been chosen as a compromise between the number of holes needed and the time taken to drill each hole, and it is now set up in the electric drill. Before starting to drill, a last look is taken inside the boot where the drill will be coming through. Oops! just as well. The cables feeding the left hand stop/tail lamps pass just below the place where the cut-outs will be. They are therefore unclipped and moved back out of harm's way.

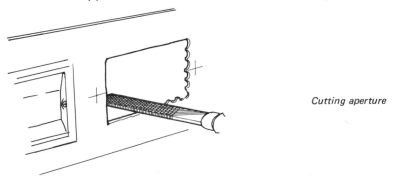

Cutting aperture

Then comes the tedious drilling of a long series of holes, followed by cutting out the centre pieces and filing the rough edges to size. A rotary file in the electric drill helps with this part of the chore. About half way through the job you come to the conclusion that surface mounted lamps that did not need such cut-outs would have looked just as nice! However, eventually the filing is finished and the lamps can be checked for fit into their cut-outs. Make sure that the centre-points for the fixing screws are still correctly aligned and that the lamps will be squarely positioned relative to the bodywork lines. Then drill the correct size holes for the self-tapping fixing screws.

Make sure that all the burrs and rough edges have been removed, and clean away all the filings and metal chippings. Remove the protective adhesive tape and clean any marks off the paintwork. Paint the cut edges of the metal. The lamps have sealing gaskets with them. Give each gasket a thin film of grease on each side, and then place it between the lamp housing and the vehicle body, and secure the lamp in position with the self-tapping screws.

Now, stand back and admire your handiwork!

Turning your attention now to the switch panel, fix the switches and pilot lamps into alternate holes. The switches are secured by removing a clamp nut from a central boss, passing this through the hole in the panel, and re-fixing the clamp nut. Make sure that all the switches are the same way up; it can be very confusing if some go up for 'on' and some go down. If you are fussy, and want them to work a particular way, check the continuity of one of the switches using a test lamp as described in Chapter 18. The pilot lamps simply clip into the holes.

Now, make up two short loops of green cable with a push-on connector on each end, to join the supply side of the three switches together. Fit push-on connectors to each of the pilot lamp leads and fit to the circuit side of the adjacent switch. The panel should now be ready for fitting, but as a check, put all three switches in the 'on' position, connect the supply side of the

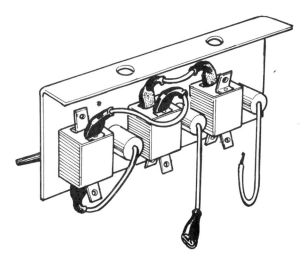

Partly wired switch panel

switches to a battery supply and touch the panel against the vehicle earthed frame. All three pilot lamps should light. If they do not, start checking to see what went wrong.

By offering up the panel, determine the most convenient position for fixing, and then mark out the centres for the fixing screws on the flange beneath the instrument panel. Centre-pop and drill for the self-tapping screws, being careful that the drill does not touch any of the existing wiring behind the panel. Screw the panel into place, and then sit and play tunes on the switches for a few minutes while you consider the next step.

Get your length of green 28/.012 cable, and from the engine compartment work it through the grommet in the bulkhead where the main wiring harness passes through. It is easier to do it from this side. Pull the end down inside until you have room to get at it to fit on a push-on connector. When this is done, push it on to the supply side of the switches on the new panel. Pull back the cable to take up the slack and secure it to the existing panel wiring with some lengths of adhesive tape. In the engine compartment cut the cable to length, fit a connector and push it on to the fuse. Tidy the job up by taping the cable onto the existing wiring harness. Check that operation of the switches lights the pilot lamps.

Check the size of the rubber grommet you have purchased, and select a drill bit about 1/16 inch larger than the hole through the grommet. With this drill make the hole through the rear bulkhead which is needed to pass the cable through. Select a position which is accessible from both sides and will give a tidy cable run. After deburring the hole, snap in the grommet.

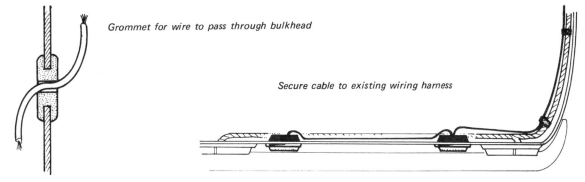

Grommet for wire to pass through bulkhead

Secure cable to existing wiring harness

Fit a connector to one end of the green/red 14/.010 cable and push it on to the pilot lamp side of the reversing lamp switch. Now, run the cable in along the planned route underneath the carpet, and thread it through the grommet. Once in the boot, tidy the cable by taping it to the existing wiring harness. Cut the cable at the correct point to reach the terminal of the first lamp and bare the end of the conductor. Do the same for one end of the remaining length of cable.

Twist the two bared ends together and secure into the lamp terminal. Cut the remaining cable end at the correct point to reach the second lamp and connect that up as well.

Operate the switch and stand back to admire your working reversing lamps. If they do not work, start checking the circuits. Poor earthing of the frame of the lamps is one likely cause of failure.

Job 2 — Silencer

The problem

Your vehicle suddenly has become very noisy. A quick look underneath shows that the exhaust system has corroded so badly that the rear end of the silencer has just broken away completely and the exhaust is nearly blowing straight through. Feeling keen you decide to tackle the replacement job yourself.

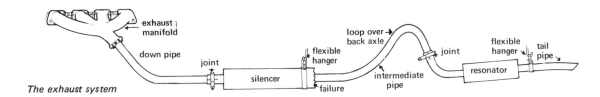

The exhaust system

First examine the exhaust system thoroughly. On this vehicle it is in three parts. A large bore pipe from a joint with the engine exhaust manifold down to a sleeve joint just in front of the silencer appears to be in pretty good condition. The second part consists of the main silencer with a length of pipe which loops upwards in a peculiar curve over the rear axle. The silencer is paper thin and would be quite unrepairable, and the pipe is badly corroded. The final section has a sleeve joint just behind the rear axle, followed by a supplementary silencer (or resonator box) and the final tail pipe. While still serviceable, this is already well eaten into by rust, and it would seem to be sensible to replace it as well as the centre section.

A visit is therefore made to your supplier to buy the appropriate two sections, together with new clamps for the sleeve joints.

Taking apart

When you are ready to start, get the vehicle on level ground and jack it up where it will give maximum accessibility for the exhaust system. Set up a pile of timber as a safety back-up for the jack and remove the rear wheel to give you maximum clearance.

Now, before you do anything else, offer up the new components alongside the old ones, and check that they look right. There are so many variants that it is easy for your supplier to give you the wrong ones.

They look all right, so move on to the next stage. Thoroughly soak all the nuts to be loosened, with penetrating oil. Squirt some onto the sleeve joints as well. While this is soaking in, use a wire brush to remove the loose rust.

Remove the rearmost sleeve joint clamp and unfasten the flexible support for the tail pipe, remembering to keep safe the bolts and nuts. Rocking the tail pipe around soon loosens it, and a few sharp blows with a hammer on the front of the resonator box pulls the joint free and the whole section can be removed.

Moving on to the middle section, again the sleeve joint clamp is removed and the intermediate flexible hanger unclipped. This one is more stubborn and the broken end to the silencer prevents any leverage being applied through the looped pipe. Indeed it is not difficult to tear out the remains of this pipe from the silencer and discard it. After some further rocking of the silencer, and hammering, it is loosened enough that it can be turned at the sleeve joint but will not pull clear.

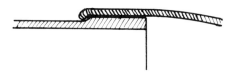

Section through corroded joint

Close examination of the joint suggests that a not uncommon effect has taken place. The inner pipe at this point is the thicker down pipe from the engine which is protected from corrosion by the outer sleeve. This outer pipe has however been corroded and weakened. Continual expansion and contraction as the pipes heat and cool results in the weaker outer pipe becoming curved at the outer end and hooked into a corroded groove formed at the edge of the joint.

This situation requires more drastic treatment, and the next action is to take a hacksaw and saw through the pipe between the joint and the silencer. With the silencer out of the way, a fine hacksaw is used to split the remaining piece of tubing so that it can be knocked free.

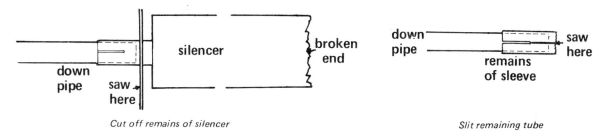

Cut off remains of silencer   *Slit remaining tube*

Putting together

Clean up the end of the front pipe after any damage caused by cutting away the old sleeve joint. De-burr the new pipes and make sure that the two parts will join together easily. This requires a bit of filing and hammering because the manufacturing tolerances are pretty rough.

Smear the end of the front pipe with 'Gun-gum' or other high-temperature jointing compound, and manoeuvre the second section of the system into place. Twisting the pipe backwards and forwards will help to fit the sleeve over the front pipe. Make sure that it is sufficiently far on for there to be no gaps showing through the slits in the end of the joint. Make sure that the looped pipe is in its correct position relative to the back axle; you do not want them hitting when you drive over a bump. Refit the flexible hanger for the silencer, and hammer around the sleeve joint to close it in. Finally, fit the new joint clamp and tighten up.

Repeat the same procedure for the rear pipe section. When it is all together, and the clamps pulled up tight, make sure that the system is free to swing on its flexible supports. Then start the engine and run it for a few minutes to warm up the pipes. Listen for any sounds of leaks from the joints. When the pipes are hot, switch off the engine and get underneath and tighten the clamps again.

Replace the rear wheel, remove the safety blocks and lower the wheel off the jack. Bounce it up and down on its springs and rev the engine, to make sure that the new exhaust system does not rattle against anything.

The tools described throughout this book are ones which you may find useful to help you in your automobile maintenance. A good workshop would probably contain most of them, together with a good workbench, store cupboard and supplies of screws, etc. You will probably make a selection which meets your own particular needs within the range of your pocket. You may also add other special proprietary gadgets which take your fancy. Their omission from this book is no condemnation of them; I have simply tried to concentrate on the widely available general purpose tools. However, you will need to carry some tools in the vehicle itself to deal with roadside emergencies, and you can hardly get the whole workshop in. This chapter, therefore, gives my suggestions for a basic tool kit for the vehicle. It represents my own personal likes and you will probably want to make your own variations.

Tools
   — Spanners, both ring and open jaw types, to match the most common size fastenings. This will probably involve about half-a-dozen double-ended spanners
   — Screwdrivers, one large and one small flat blade, and at least one cross type blade
   — Spark plug spanner
   — Small/medium size pair of pliers
   — Toggle grip pliers ('Mole-grip')
   — A broken hacksaw blade, preferably with a handle
   — A medium size engineer's hammer

Materials
   — A small selection of nuts, bolts and washers
   — A few feet of electric cable (in case of a need to reconnect something)
   — One or two feet of steel wire (for securing broken parts)
   — A piece of asbestos gasket material (for emergency replacement of a blown gasket)
   — A roll of adhesive PVC or similar tape, about 1 inch wide. This can be used for insulating electrical connections, securing loose components, or repairing a leaking water hose
   — A pack of epoxy resin adhesive ('Araldite')
   — Some paper towels for mopping up the vehicle and yourself

Spare parts
   The actual components to be carried will depend very much on the vehicle and your probable proximity to a supplier. Take special note of any feature of the vehicle which is uncommon. It is gratifying to own an automobile which incorporates the latest developments, but remember that Joe Blogg's 'Old Smithy Garage' in Much Binding may not stock the necessary replacement part. If you fit new components, the old ones may still have enough life in them to be worth carrying as emergency spares.

Likely items to be considered are:

— Fuses
— Bulbs, especially tail and head lights
— Spark plug
— Fan belt
— Camshaft drive belt (if fitted)
— Contact breaker points and condenser

Kit bag

All of these items need to be herded together in some manner. A plastic or metal tool box may be all right in the workshop, but it tends to be a bit noisy and bulky in the boot of the car. prefer a tool roll made from strong canvas or thin leather. Some people prefer a small hold-all bag. Whatever you use, do not forget to give all the tools a film of oil or grease to avoid rusting.

Other items

As well as the tools themselves, there are a number of other items which should be carried on the vehicle:

— Tyre pressure gauge
— Plastic scraper for de-icing windows. You may prefer to add one of the spray-on de-icing fluids
— Clean lint free duster for keeping the interior of windows clean and free from condensation
— First aid kit
— Fire extinguisher
— Warning triangle (to be placed in road behind broken down vehicle to warn oncoming traffic)
— Tow rope
— A pair of heavy battery 'jumper' cables with spring clips on each end. If your battery is flat, these will allow you to borrow a 'start' from someone else's battery
— A torch or battery lantern

Chapter 27 Where to Get Things

Information

The first thing you need to get is information. Start off by buying a workshop manual for your automobile. I do not mean the driver's handbook issued with the vehicle, which varies from being quite useful to little more than advice to 'take it to your dealer'. No, the one you want is one of the very comprehensive specialist books used by garages themselves. Sometimes the vehicle manufacturer will publish such a book and make it available to customers; more often you will have to rely on a commercial publisher. Do not pick the cheapest; buy the most comprehensive one; it will be worth it. J. H. Haynes and Company offer a good range of such manuals.

Borrow books on automobile maintenance from your local library and get yourself thoroughly immersed in the subject. Take out a subscription for one of the regular motoring magazines, such as *Practical Motorist, Autocar or Motor*. They will provide you with a steady supply of useful hints and advertisements of all the latest gadgets.

Check up on how much your neighbours know; you may have a specialist nearby or someone with useful contacts. If you are feeling really keen, consider joining a local or one make motor club. There you will always find someone willing to help with your problems.

Materials and facilities

Try to establish a good relationship with a smallish local garage. Trade there regularly and get yourself accepted as a good customer. Then when you have a problem you cannot cope with, or need some special facility, you will be likely to get sympathetic attention.

You must of course get to know the main dealer holding the local franchise for your make of vehicle. His stores will be the source of many of your spare parts.

Check your local trade directory for specialist suppliers and service facilities. It is common practice to find firms specialising in auto-electrics, carburettors, tyres, suspension components, brakes, exhaust systems, bodywork and painting, engine tuning, and supplying proprietary components. The main purpose of these firms is usually to supply a service to the garage trade, but if you know what you want, and it is in their line, they are usually just as happy to serve you. The quality of service you will get is usually better than that from a general maintenance facility and likely to be cheaper. You must be sure, however, that you do know exactly what you want to do; if you are not too happy to take the responsibility for putting the bits together, you will just have to pay someone else to do it for you.

Many of the multiple stores, in particular Boots and Halfords, stock materials and components specially selected for the do-it-yourself automobile maintainer. You will also need to locate a good ironmongers or engineer's supplies shop to provide for your needs in the nuts, bolts, oils, etc line. You may be lucky enough to locate in your neighbourhood a 'speed shop' which caters specifically for the automobile accessory, maintenance and tuning market. It is worth travelling quite a way to find a good one of these.

Buying parts

Before you visit your supplier, be quite sure that you know what you are going for. Make a complete shopping list. Be sure that you know the correct description for components. It is often worth taking your vehicle manual with you so that you can point to the component you need on a drawing. Main dealer's stores usually have illustrated parts cataglogues which can help in identifying components.

Be sure that you know what vehicle you have got. Take along details of maker, model name, engine size, if it has automatic transmission, type of bodywork, month and year of delivery, engine number and chassis number. The last two are vital as last resort checks; sometimes you will find that a particular design of component was fitted on only a few hundred vehicles. When you do get the components home, offer them up into position if you can, to see if they look as if they will fit.

I hope that this book will help you to carry out the maintenance work on your automobile with such great efficiency that you will never be afflicted by troubles. However, life being what it is, the day will probably come when you are broken down, miles from anywhere, without the right tools or spare parts. So, for the finishing touch, here are an assortment of ideas for emergency 'codge-ups' which may help you on that occasion when it comes.

Unsuitable tools

If you have not got the size of spanner you need, you may be able to get by with a size larger by inserting the blade of a screwdriver to act as a wedge. Or alternatively, there is always the possibility of using a pair of pliers or a toggle-grip.

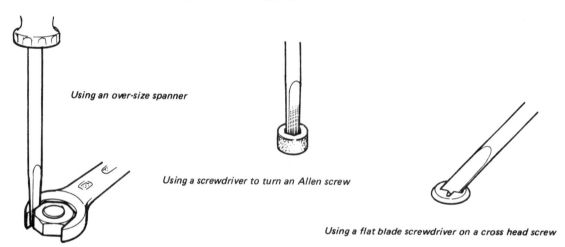

Using an over-size spanner

Using a screwdriver to turn an Allen screw

Using a flat blade screwdriver on a cross head screw

If you need to move a socket head screw and you have no Allen keys with you, a screwdriver blade wedged into the hexagon may meet your need.

Similarly, a flat blade screwdriver can be adapted to fit a cross-drive screw head if used with care. Of course, for all of these the amount of leverage you will have will not be very great.

If you should need to make a hole in metalwork, when you have not got a drill with you, the following method will work if the metal is not too thick. Punch a hole first, using a small screwdriver hit by a hammer. Twisting the screwdriver will open up the hole and this can be followed by a large size screwdriver or the tang of a file used as a reamer.

If the thread on a screw is stripped, there may be situations where a size smaller bolt with a nut can be used as a replacement.

Non-available spares

A broken fan belt has been replaced before now with a nylon stocking tied around the pulleys. However this situation, like many others, is one where you can manage without if you are very careful. Many automobiles can dispense with their cooling fan except for long idling on very hot days. The big snag is that the fan belt usually also drives the generator and water pump. The generator you can manage without for hours if you do not use headlamps and other heavy electrical loads. You can manage without the cooling water pump for a few miles if you drive gently and stop occasionally to let the water cool down.

Similarly, if a cooling water hose breaks and you cannot repair the burst, just blank the hose off. Interior heater hoses of course are no problem; the main hoses to top and bottom of the radiator are a different matter. With one out of circuit, you are relying on the static mass of water trapped in the engine block to keep it cool. With care you may be able to limp to a garage. To blank off a hose, disconnect one end, or cut it in half and fold the hose back on itself. Pinch this fold shut with a twist of wire. If you break a hose clip, a serviceable substitute can be made

To seal a hose pipe

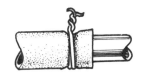

Emergency hose clip

by taking a length of wire, wrapping it around the end of the hose, and twisting the wire ends together. Use as many strands of wire as necessary to get the strength you need.

Hydraulic brakes may fail by getting a leak in one of the brake cylinders or in one of the flexible hoses. Cut the faulty brake out of circuit by pinching off the brake hose using a 'Mole Grip'. Top up the system, if necessary, by using ordinary oil, or even water, if the correct fluid is not available. But remember to clean it all out when the repair is made later.

If you need a spare fuse and you have forgotten to get some, the following trick can be used. Make sure, of course, that you first remove the fault which caused the fuse to blow, and that you fit a proper replacement later. Cut a piece of stranded cable from your emergency kit; remove the insulation and extract a number of strands. Pick sufficient so that their total thickness looks about as thick as the remnants of wire in the fuse. Wrap the strands around the blown fuse so that when it is clipped back in the wires are held.

Temporary fuse

If a component has failed in such a way that it is probably a write-off anyway, do not hesitate to use it further if it will help to get you to civilisation. For example, a broken ball in a ball bearing will make sufficient noise to make you stop and investigate. Once you have identified the cause, make sure that excessive play in the bearing will not cause damage elsewhere, and then carry on slowly. The rest of the bearing will be wrecked eventually, but it has to be changed anyway.

Do not overlook the strength and resilience of green timber. A branch cut from a neighbouring tree can make a good splint for a broken member. Even if you break a suspension spring, it may be possible to wedge it with a piece of timber. You will have to drive very carefully, but it can get you to a garage.